The Defined Contribution Handbook

An Inside Guide to Service Providers & Advisors

By Keith Clark

Foreword by Nevin E. Adams,
Plan Sponsor magazine

MARKETPLACE BOOKS
Columbia, MD

This book, along with other books, are available at discounts that make it realistic to provide them as gifts to your customers, clients and staff. For more information on these long-lasting, cost-effective premiums, please call John Boyer at 800-272-2855 or e-mail him at john@fpbooks.com.

ISBN 1-59280-062-9

Printed in the United States of America

Table of Contents

CHAPTER VI

CHAPTER VII

CHAPTER VIII

CHAPTER IX

Foreword

"Truth" and Consequences

OK, true confession — I've been a recordkeeper — and I liked it.

What's a recordkeeper? Well, odds are if you are reading this book (not to mention this foreword), you already know. But for the uninitiated, a recordkeeper is the guy (or gal) who helps make sure the retirement savings statement is right. Fifteen years ago they were doing it with 12-column pads and green eyeshades — today with a keyboard and dynamic HTML displays. Fundamentally it is the process of making sure that the right numbers go into the right "buckets."

What numbers? That money that gets pulled out of your paycheck every payday, for one thing. That money your employer puts in on your behalf — and the earnings that accumulate — or detract from — those amounts. Recordkeepers calculate how much money you have, figure out if you can have a loan (and for how much), and — when the time comes — tell the Internal Revenue Service how much tax you owe on the money you have saved for retirement.

Pretty heady stuff, huh?

Actually, no. For the most part, it's a thankless job—and that's on the good days.

The Bottom Lines

First off, unlike most jobs (save brain surgery), you are expected to do it perfectly 100% of the time — just to be *average*. That requires smart people and expensive technology — which is costly. Retirement plans pay hundreds of thousands of dollars in investment management fees with nary a thought, because those fees are netted against assets. Yet, recordkeeping has always been a service that employers must write a check for — and they *hate* writing those checks.

7

Worse yet, while good recordkeepers frequently attract the opportunity to manage money (in spite of poor returns), the guys *managing* the money get all the glory. So, while investment management fees blossom, and their stars make the cover of industry publications and *Fortune* — when was the last time you saw a recordkeeper on the cover of ANY publication?

Still, ask any plan sponsor who has struggled through a painful conversion, any participant who has waited weeks for that desperately needed 401(k) distribution check — and they'll tell you that a good recordkeeper is worth — well, a lot more than they are getting paid.

Of course, that's part of the fun of being a recordkeeper. To borrow from an old Army adage, knowing that you do more before 9 a.m. than most do all day, makes it worthwhile. It's a black box to most — but it's our black box.

So how does one become a recordkeeper? Well it helps to have a fondness for detail (not to be confused with neatness), a love of numbers, an affinity for solving puzzles, a streak of masochism — and the ability to work productively for long hours with no sleep. Recordkeepers aren't born, they are made, as you will discover when reading Keith's new book.

The Devil's in the Details

A word of warning — as Otto van Bismark famously once said, "Laws are like sausages; it is better *not* to see them being made." And, laws have nothing on the process of participant recordkeeping. So, if you're not into details, you might consider skipping over the first few chapters. It's great background — nothing like knowing where the business has been to appreciate how far it's come. But perhaps not for the faint-hearted.

Fishermen have their fish tales, and every recordkeeper has at least one "horror story" . . . one "snake bit" client that just couldn't go right . . . one hard-to-deliver sales commitment to a potential client. What this industry has needed for a long time — and Keith has managed to do — is make sense of all the wrongs, the errors and the misunderstandings about recordkeeping. His new work provides some frank, much needed insight into how the defined contribution industry operates, so those making choices and advising clients can be armed with the best knowledge available to base decisions on. More importantly, he shows not just what goes wrong — or can go wrong — but all the things that can, and do, go right.

Foreword

At *Plan Sponsor* magazine it is our mission to keep the advising community fully informed and aware of every new event affecting the industry. We cover in detail service providers, plan sponsors and participants, and a vast array of plans themselves. When new developments occur, we try to be the first to unveil them. Such is the case with Keith Clark's groundbreaking new book. It's truly one of the first pieces to provide an inside peek into the operations of both service providers and the decision making process, illustrating how those decisions are often made at the expense of the participants. Reading this book will educate all parties involved on how the system really works, so they can make informed decisions regarding their company and their clients. Anyone operating in this arena today will benefit from the candor and inside perspective Keith Clark provides.

If you're a plan sponsor, this book will tell you things you may not want to know — but should. As Keith illustrates, no plan sponsor task so dramatically — and immediately — affects perceptions of the plan as recordkeeping. Even strong fund performance is of little value if you can't associate it with an account balance.

If you're an investment advisor, reading this book can save you time and money, as you discover that nothing will sour — or solidify — a relationship with your client quicker than the quality of your recordkeeper. Find it out the *hard* way — or the easier way with this book.

Finally, if you're reading this book as a recordkeeper — God bless you. You'll be thrilled someone has finally put into writing what you've seen and known for years. And while you're at it, pick up some extra copies. You'll want to get:

- one for your parents so they can finally understand what it is you do (and explain it to their friends)
- one for your spouse and kids — maybe it will give them an appreciation for what those late nights and missed soccer games were really all about
- one for that boss who always had to step out during your presentation
- one for your clients — each of them — complete with underlined passages.

But make sure you keep a copy for yourself — you've earned it!

— Nevin E. Adams
Editor, *Plan Sponsor* magazine

Introduction

Both the best and the worst day of my entire 16-year career in the defined-contribution industry was when I left the grind of record-keeping administration of employee-benefit plans. In the days immediately following, I felt relieved, like a school kid on the first day of summer break, that I no longer had to track an exhaustive 'To Do' list for my clients and internal operations. I'm sure those of you in this industry can relate. But, I also felt like I was abandoning the hardworking people in our industry, over 500 of whom I had personally recruited. I was witness to many funny episodes, horrifying errors and hidden agendas, and shared a lifetime of experiences with these dedicated record keepers and human-resource executives. I know, firsthand, the sacrifices these people make to ensure that nothing slips through the cracks.

Record-keeping administration can be summarized in a variety of ways, but primarily as a thankless industry, since perfection is the expected 'norm.' It also features low profits and high stress because, of course, it is always the record keeper's fault when something goes wrong in the plan.

Since leaving my post as a record keeper, I have studied Process Management at Auburn University as part of their masters program, and have combined my 16 years of record-keeping administration experience with my studies to help service firms meet their strategic objectives (or better get them). I have worked with over 100 record keepers on their process management and the challenges of plan compliance, investment industry integration, trust reporting/audits, individual plan nuances, participant communications, and the zero- defect tolerance. Over the years, I have discovered that five trends are always present:

1. Record-keeping service providers often sell a brand-new service before it is built, and build it after the business is awarded to them.

2. With more technology, it seems there are more errors, not less. Why? Because our industry is becoming more automated and trusting technology too much. The good news in today's technology is that errors are caught almost immediately, thereby reducing major liability from a dollar perspective; however, it still tarnishes the service providers' credibility.

3. Record keepers tell a good story about their management and operation structure, but in reality many managers may be excellent in reacting to client issues, but are horrendous at proactive management to make sure their companies are appropriately staffed, with the right level of controls. The issue is that our business does not accept managers who simply manage; they have to be able to record keep, and are not looked upon highly by their team if they are not performing some record-keeping work. In other words, record keepers tend to hold onto their 'sacred cows' or old way of doing things.

4. Human Resource departments are constantly asked to sharpen their budget pencils, while, at the same time, providing more services to their employees. The impact to the defined-contribution plan is generally that the participants pay more, albeit indirectly.

5. New laws are introduced or existing laws are revised that cause significant changes in systems and processes. Such laws, whether necessary or not, are often seemingly enacted without any real understanding by the lawmakers of the impact they will ultimately have on the industry. Accommodating even small changes in the law may drive up the cost of providing services, because entire record-keeping systems must be reprogrammed.

How does one get into this business, and why would anyone sign up for a business where you have to "eat nails for breakfast?"

Certainly no one grows up dreaming of being a human resources or defined-contributions expert. Most of us enter this business because it is related to computers or investments. In early 1986, I was a young graduate of the University of Minnesota with ambitions of ruling the world before I was 25. I was hired, by Hewitt Associates, as a record-keeping administrator responsible for updating participant accounts. I, like everyone else, was ambitious and fired up that I was making over $22,000 a year. I told my parents I was rich.

Introduction

I also had no idea what business I was getting into, other than that Hewitt Associates was one of the best companies to work for (still is today), and they offered a free lunch (and still do!). No one knew what a 401(k) plan was at that time (although with all of the press, we sure do today). As a side note, there weren't, and still aren't, any degrees in Employee Benefits offered at the collegiate level. Now we have organizations such as CEBS, SPARK, NIPA, and ASPA that provide professional designations and fantastic industry updates, but it is mostly legal and compliance matter. To this day, very few firms have managers dedicated to process management in our industry, which is a cornerstone of a record-keeping service provider's success.

To make a long story short, I started off as a record-keeping processor and within one year, my peers and managers realized how much havoc a renegade without much processing or legal knowledge could cause. In my first year, I sent out quarterly statements with incorrect earnings, incorrect company names, and worse yet, I still had no idea what a trust-to-records reconciliation was. This is probably the most important job a record-keeping administrator has, as it reconciles all of the participant accounts to the monies actually invested in the trust, by fund, within the plan.

The point is, this business can bring even the brightest people to their knees. It requires strong organizational skills. Most importantly, the record-keeping service providers must provide an environment that fosters new employees, and allows them to learn at their own pace. Again, process management (including training) is the key to success, and there are very few record-keeping service provider firms that have this figured out.

For those of you who manage, or sell, in this business, and are new to the industry, it takes at least 2-3 years of experience before you can become fluent. But, if you have the tenacity to stick with it, it really is a fun and rewarding industry. Having said that, those new to the industry are the best ones to point out better ways to process the data and serve the client (hopefully your manager is not "old school," and is willing to change).

To this day, I still meet accountants and senior executives of plan sponsors who proclaim that record keeping is simply bookkeeping. These uninformed opinions are what mislead people about our industry. And, I have found investment advisors, brokers, and investment managers who claim record keeping is a trivial component of the defined-contribution equation. Again, this thinking could not be further from the truth. If record-keeping administration is that easy, then why do we have less than ten record-keeping software systems supporting the thousands of record-keeping service providers? The answer is that it's NOT easy to create software systems that encompass:

- Plan compliance (innumerable regulations, tests, and compliance forms)
- Integration with the investment industry
- Trust reporting/Audits of plans
- Participant communications

Or, that allow for:

- The stress of having to work in a zero-defect environment
- Virtually every plan having its own nuances

A little history lesson is in order to demonstrate the importance of process and ethics. Back in the mid-1980s, most plans were updated on a quarterly, or annual basis, as this was the common frequency of updating 401(k) accounts. Even back then, people would ask why we couldn't update their 401(k) account every day, when their local bank could update their bank accounts each day. In the pre-mutual-fund days, record-keeping systems were inflexible, as they were built for compliance. Record keepers essentially recorded what happened in the investment funds or trust accounts, after the quarter occurred. Yes, a lot can actually happen during that quarter when no one is watching, and when participants and plan sponsors send their transaction requests via paper.

Here are just a few examples:

EXAMPLE 1: An Old-Time Story
Many of us take for granted that if you want to transfer your monies in your 401(k) account today, all you have to do is log onto the Internet or call a 1-800 number. Back in the old days, participant transfers were offered once a quarter, and you had to complete a form at least 5 business days before the end of the quarter. This was not only a lot of pressure to place on a participant (only being able to transfer quarterly and on a specific date), but was also tremendous pressure for the record-keeping service provider since the accounts were only

updated four times a year, and, typically not until 15-30 business days after quarter-end.

We had to perform the transfers on the first day of the new quarter on an estimated basis, based on the previous quarter's balance and estimating the earnings for the quarter (this was in the days when investment managers did not release performance numbers for up to 5 days following quarter-end). The problem arose when the record-keeping service provider forgot to perform these estimated transfers, thereby assuming, by default, the role of investment manager. You would be surprised how many record-keeping service providers did not estimate the transfers, hence playing the market with the plan's money. Simply by not transferring $100,000 from the money-market fund to an aggressive equity fund, for example, could result in the plan and the participant missing out on one month's worth of earnings (or getting lucky if the fund went down during that period).

In the old days, most plans did not process in a share environment where the participant knew how many shares they held in a mutual fund. Any errors made by the record-keeping service provider affected the return of the funds involved, and almost every participant either benefited or lost because of this. If you only knew how many times these errors went unreported, with the gain or loss in the funds passed on to the entire plan. For those of us in the industry, we dreaded the calculation of comparing what should have happened in the investment funds to what actually occurred, before sending participant statements.

Ironically, for those providers that did perform this important calculation, if there were large discrepancies, they had the choice of changing the record-keeping system OR just telling the client it was due to timing. What's worse is the number of record-keeping service providers that did not even perform this proof and control. I am sure many of you have seen statements with negative earnings in a money-market fund, when that is virtually impossible. For the record, there was nothing better than that feeling of finding out your error added monies to the plan. The worst feeling was what happened when it went the other way. (The best firms take responsibility and are honest with their clients.)

Now you know why a lot of us have gray hair.

EXAMPLE 2: Today's Dreaded Error

Take the same example as above, and apply it to today's environment. When a plan sponsor decides to switch record-keeping service providers, I can't tell you how many of those providers hold the converted monies in money-market funds until the participant records from the previous record keeper are sent. What does this mean? The same as above: the new record-keeping service provider has made an unauthorized investment decision on behalf of the plan participants, during the conversion period (which can last anywhere from 1 to 45 business days). Ironically, this is another issue that does not need to occur. The new record-keeping service provider can simply map the monies into the new funds, or estimate the monies based on their new investment elections. We will explain this process, in depth, in Chapter III.

EXAMPLE 3: What can happen when no one is minding the store?

What happens to the money if rollovers, employee contributions, or loan repayments are not invested in the plan trust on a timely basis? For a weekly payroll, if a record keeper and/or its bank takes an extra day to process and update an employee contribution, you will have missed 52 days of investment performance, by the end of a year.

Who gets the earnings in this case? It depends on who is holding the money and how they are holding it. Some record-keeping service providers and their bank (directed trustee) invest it in money-market funds on the plan's behalf, which is allocated to all participants. Others hold the money in an overnight account, whereby the service provider can benefit (when asked about who gets the earnings, the answer is often that it is incorporated into their fee). Even with conversion monies, one day can make a difference.

EXAMPLE 4: Why are ethics the key to the success?

In our business, ethics play a key role in the success of the plan. In all of the above examples, when confronted with the issue, or when the issue occurs, the first thought a record keeper may have is, "Can I bury the error?" Even the best administrators may have a natural reflex to think this, but the ethical firms in the business admit all of their errors without even batting an eye (regardless of the tolerance levels accepted by the industry).

When errors occur, it's a terrible feeling and the record keeper, alone, must call the client, as well as tell the boss. Each person in the company feels badly, because they have a write-off coming, AND they are jeopardizing future revenues with that client. The client contact is upset when told, because they have to tell not only their boss, but also their participants, which could have a major impact on morale. If an investment advisor or broker is involved, they will immediately fear they are losing their revenue because of the record-keeping error.

Ironically, in an environment that updates accounts daily, you will rarely hear of the errors that have a positive impact on the plan. As a record keeper, try this phone call to the client: "By the way, we screwed up your plan for the third time this year, and luckily, for the third time, it turned out to help the plan." That is not going to fly and you are going to lose your client, even though the errors turned out for the best, because it creates doubt in your ability to serve.

By the way, the tolerance zone for errors varies depending upon the transaction (usually less than a basis point, or 1/100th of one percent). Before you run and check your last ten years' worth of participant statements, the good news is that many of today's plans are performed in a share-accounting environment. This simply means that for each contribution or dividend allocated, you are allocated shares in the fund. It is virtually impossible to hide an error in share accounting, as the record keeper has to sell your shares to account for the error. Trust me on this one; with the advent of technology, more people are tracking their retirement plans on a spreadsheet or popular tracking program. They will know, hence it will not happen, which is one of the best audit values in the business (it is free, however the public relations hit to the company is not). In fact, many of these people drive plan sponsors crazy if the plan is not in a share-accounting environment.

I have often told people that have saved their participant statements over the years that they will come across a windfall in earnings, or a significant loss, as compared to the actual returns for certain quarters, especially back in the 1980s and early 1990s (the pre-mutual-fund years). Yes, this may spur many retirees, or accountants, with time on their hands to check and see if their accounts were updated correctly. It is not a bad move, however it may be tough to get earnings figures for non-mutual funds unless you are willing to dig hard enough.

Where is this book taking us?

As I continue to work and enjoy working in the industry, I recognize the need for a reference manual or guidebook discussing process management, integrating technology, profitability, and plan design, as much to enlighten peripheral service entities as for the record-keeping administrators themselves. From time to time, I began drafting such a text, but every time I was close to finishing, there would be new technology, legislation or products that needed to be added.

After reviewing my most recent attempt, my editor commented that it seemed like I was holding something back. As we discussed my approach, it became apparent that I had tried to shield certain players in this industry — playing politics to a small degree. While I covered virtually every angle of servicing a defined-contribution plan in an easy to understand manner, I had withheld valuable truths that could make the difference between success and failure.

What now follows on these pages is a "no holds barred" presentation. What once were the dirty little secrets in the business are exposed, along with a process for how to leverage this information.

As you study this material, you must first understand that profits in the defined-contribution industry are easier to achieve through the investment transaction aspect, and consulting, than as a plan sponsor or a record-keeping service provider. Yet, the role of plan sponsor or record-keeping administrator carries all the culpability. This could be likened to the airline industry, where very few carriers today are profitable, but the ancillary service industries are.

Secondly, it is important to realize that garnering what profits are to be made by the various record-keeping service providers should be as high a priority for the long-term success of their companies, as is ensuring their clients will not face any plan regulatory issues. During the hiring process of the record-keeping service provider, lowest cost for the maximum number of services has been the primary criteria. (This is ironic, since a company would not search for corporate counsel based on price, but by reputation of reducing risk/liability.) Therefore, from a record-keeper's perspective, the implementation of process management is of utmost importance. Without this foundation, it is difficult, if not impossible, to deliver excellence at a competitive price. The implementation process is important for the low-cost provider, but it is just as important for the firms focusing on premium service.

Third, and most importantly, the plan participant (employee) will become recognized as the primary client for whose benefit our services ultimately exist!

The premise of this book is not to scare the reader about the record-keeping industry. In fact, my intention is simply to provide an inside look at the defined-contribution record-keeping industry.

In this book, we will take an in-depth look at the following:

- Hidden fees and revenues—Are certain firms and individuals taking advantage of participants? Is our industry migrating to no out-of-pocket fees, all at the expense of the participant's retirement account, simply because the plan sponsor does not want to have an expense on their corporate budget? This book will give you all of the information you need about all of the fees and the investment industry.
- All service perspectives of record-keeping administration (administrators, trustees, record-keeping software, etc.)
- The plan-sponsor perspective: how a plan sponsor (company with a retirement plan) rates and should select a consultant, advisor, and service provider(s)
- How to build a successful record-keeping practice (which will really show the plan sponsor what goes on at their record keeper's shop)
- The future of the industry (it will only grow)
- Recognizing the ultimate client (the employee)

Virtually every other book written for the industry focuses on enhancing only one of these segments, or deals with the one subject at very macro levels. As I have been involved in every aspect of this industry at one time or another, my goal with this book is to demystify all roles and operational elements involved. I have strived to provide a comprehensive approach to integrating all these services to support one another for the optimum performance and profit of all parties. This material should enable record-keeping service providers to build a successful business model, and to make better business judgments, short and long term. It will provide all related providers with a better understanding of how best to utilize record-keeping administration and, potentially, with a better appreciation for the complexities these administrators regularly face. Most importantly, it will help plan sponsors build the right plan for their employees.

The defined-contribution industry is a fast-changing environment that can be rewarding for each of us who share a commitment to excellence. The companies that will profit are those that continue to invest in new, proven technologies and implement operationally efficient processes that result in an excellent work environment, as well as provide the highest level of quality to the plan participant.

Acknowledgements

I have written this book as a way to acknowledge all the record-keeping administrators and human resource professionals who have spent countless hours burning the midnight oil and missing important family functions and vacations to serve their client, the plan participant. Your Herculean efforts usually go unthanked; yet, you play one of the most important roles in participants' lives; that is, helping them achieve their realistic retirement goals and better manage their current employee benefits.

The book is also written to enlighten the investment advisors and brokers. This book may give you your first look inside a record-keeping shop and insight into what actually goes on there.

Special thanks go to Larry Chambers (editor), Pete Kirtland (helping on the ASP Model section), Amy Cavanaugh (writing the first draft of the Compliance section, and she is one of the best compliance consultants in the industry), Karen Turner (reading and rewriting my first drafts), and Nevin Adams. My partner, Doug Hoefer deserves an extra special thanks, as he has read every draft in the last three years and can probably recite the book verbally by now. Finally, the entire team at Marketplace Books deserves the ultimate thanks for the wonderful job pulling this book together.

Most importantly, it is my hope that my family and friends will now understand what I have been up to for all of these years, especially my two sons, Brandon and Sammy. If you do not read any further in this book, please know that I have learned that being passionate about serving your clients is fantastic, but not at the expense of your family. It is your faith and family that come first.

CHAPTER I

A Layman's View of Industry Terminology and History

Throughout the history of this industry, the players have often been called upon to wear multiple hats, interchanging them minute by minute. Many of us have "grown up" in the business and evolved into our current roles after rummaging around in various positions, finding our forte.

To the outside observer, let alone the neophyte, it could be confusing and difficult to sort out. The definitions below are offered as much to put us all on the same page in the discussions presented in this book, as they are for clarification. Therefore, if you are a veteran, skip this chapter and move on to the juicy stuff in Chapter II, such as the inside look at fees, from hidden to disclosed.

First, let's look at a "hierarchy" chart (*see* figure 1 on next page) of the industry illustrating how the industry's primary responsibility is to the plan participant.

Basic Plan-Sponsor Terminology

Defined-Contribution Plans — Retirement savings/investment plans offered by public and private companies, including government agencies. They allow the participant to make their own investment decisions based on the plan's menu. Although frequently lumped under the singular description of 401(k) in the popular press, the basic plan types are:

- Profit Sharing
- Money Purchase
- Employee Stock Ownership
- 401(k)

Figure 1. Defined Contribution Service Hierarchy

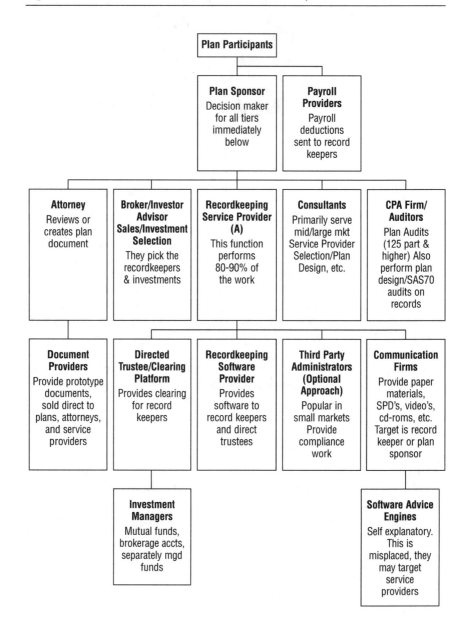

Defined-Benefit Plans — "Pension" plans that are managed by the company (or whomever they hire to manage the assets), and provide the participant an income guarantee at retirement, based on years of service and salary.

Plan Sponsors — The company, government group, or entity offering a defined-contribution plan

Plan Participants — Employees of the plan sponsor who are eligible and elect to participate (invest money) in the defined-contribution plan via payroll deduction

The Five Key Defined-Contribution Services (provided to plan sponsors and their participants)

1. **Record-Keeping Administration** — The heart and soul of the services provided to the plan sponsor, as this portion of the plan represents over 80% of the work related to the plan. A detailed description of services is provided in the next section of this chapter, under Record-Keeping Service Providers.

2. **Directed-Trustee Services** — The firm that performs the buying and selling of the plan assets on behalf of the participants. The directed trustee is responsible for investing monies in an accurate and timely manner. The reason they are called 'directed' is that they take all direction from the record-keeping service provider, and are not responsible for any investment decisions on behalf of the plan or participant. The directed trustee holds the assets on behalf of the plan sponsor (in aggregate, not at the participant level) and is in fact contracted by the plan sponsor (not the record-keeping service provider).

3. **Participant Communications** — All of the information about the defined-contribution plan, and planning for retirement, that is provided to help the participant make ongoing deferral and investment decisions. Standard communications include Internet information, paper materials, and on-site presentations.

4. **Investments** — The fund menu the participants can select from to invest their assets. Most plans offer 8-12 mutual funds to choose from, and some plans even offer a brokerage solution. This is the driving force to the success of the participants, because they are limited to this investment menu. If the funds selected do not meet prudent standards, the record-keeping

23

service provider, investment advisor, and /or consultant may get fired and face future litigation for not performing their duties appropriately. This is the most important component of the five key services.

5. Compliance — All of the required testing mandated by our government to retain qualified status, including annual reporting via a Form 5500.

Third Party Administrator (TPA) — These firms only perform the compliance service. Although many in the industry use this term loosely, these firms do not perform the day-to-day record-keeping administration of updating the participants' accounts. In addition, the acronym TPA is often used in the health-care sector of employee-benefit plans, and is confusing to the plan sponsor.

Outsourcing — A term that is used loosely, and often incorrectly, in the marketplace that means the record-keeping service provider is handling all participant inquiries and transactions, including the approval of distributions, loans, and withdrawals, but does not include providing legal services.

Total Benefits Outsourcing — Outsourcing in which the service provider handles all defined-contribution, defined benefit, and health & welfare services for the plan sponsor and participant; but, does not include legal work or claims processing for health and dental claims (although some firms do include this). The participant goes to one site or service provider for all benefit transactions and inquiries.

Daily Valuation — The term used to describe how frequently a participant's account is updated. The most efficient and fastest way to update a participant's account is same day/late day; however, there are still plans that are valued on a daily basis that are updated the next morning, with trades often pending over a 1-3 day period.

Balance Forward — (In my opinion, the most ridiculous term ever invented.) This refers to all plans that are not updated daily, whereby participant accounts are updated monthly, quarterly, or annually. I refer to these plans as traditional, as the term implies that all other plans are *balance backward* (which many of us would like when the markets are down). ESOP (Employee Stock Option) plans and one-fund money-purchase plans are plans that are generally updated in a traditional environment.

Same Day/Late Day Trade Processing—This method is the creation of the NSCC (National Securities Clearing Corporation), a not-for-profit subsidiary of the DTC (Depository Trust Company) that settles all equity transactions on Wall Street. This process reduces operation flow by 30%–50%, hence the record-keeping service provider could become more profitable by simply shifting a plan to this approach if their fees remained constant (and if performed efficiently).

The same day/late day (SD/LD) trading platform allows plan participants to submit transfer requests right up until the market closes (4:00 p.m. EST) for plans with multiple fund families participating on the NSCC platform. The record keeper then processes the trades that evening at that day's close. Participants who requested a transfer before 4:00 p.m. (when the stock market is open) will be able to log in that evening to see their transfer completed. The record keeper actually performs the trades on the record-keeping system before the trade occurs at the mutual fund level.

Same Day/Late Day Processing

Here is how it works:

Market Closes	4:00 p.m. EST
Record keeping receives pricing input	6:30 p.m. EST
Record keeper completes updates for that day's activities and replenishes IVR and Internet for updated account balances	8:00 p.m. EST
Record keeper forwards trades to bank/clearinghouse	8:35 p.m. EST
Bank/Clearinghouse records entries and forward to NSCC for actual trading	10:00 p.m. EST
Mutual funds settle trades	Next morning

The trades at the mutual fund level are performed *after* the bell (the official market close), by the record keeper. Of course, the record keeper signs strict agreements with each mutual-fund provider that ensures the record keeper accepts no trades after that day's close.

25

Straight-Through Processing—A process that is untouched by human intervention. In our industry, many advertise this, but most can not prove it, as inevitability somewhere during the process a human is keying something into a system or shuffling paper. An example of straight through processing can best be described in the payroll process. It would run like this:

- Plan Sponsor sends or inputs the payroll/census information
- The recordkeeping system scrubs the data to ensure it matches the control totals (input by the plan sponsor or provided on the file download)
- Plan Sponsor wires the monies to the bank, directed trustee, or record-keeper
- The recordkeeping system sends a file with the investment instructions that matches the wire to the bank, directed trustee, or clearing unit (within the recordkeeper)
- The bank, directed trustee, or clearing unit invests the monies upon receipt

Some firms proclaim this process is straight through, however I have yet to see it where a human is not involved with an email, phone call, proof and control, or key entry (especially at the wire receipt/investment level or the initial scrubbing of the recordkeeping data).

Record-Keeping Service Provider History and Terminology

Who is in the record-keeping business?

The answer is almost every financial service provider, most with the goal of garnering assets under management. Each record-keeping service provider has its own target market in relation to plan size, complexity, region, and or partnerships. Following is a list of providers who offer recordkeeping administration, by industry, with generalizations:

- **Mutual-fund companies**—generally a bundled provider approach, with an emphasis on their investment funds
- **Banks**—generally offer a bundled approach, with an emphasis on their investment funds and alliance funds

- **Consulting firms** — generally offer an unbundled approach that emphasizes flexibility in investments and plan design
- **Third-party administrators** — similar to consulting firms, with the exception that the primary line of business is record-keeping administration
- **Brokerage firms** — generally offer a combination of their proprietary approach or consulting firms or TPAs, with their strength in fund selection, communication delivery, and monitoring the investments.
- **Insurance firms** — generally offer a bundled approach with an emphasis on their investment funds; traditionally offering a low or no-cost solution for start-up or small plans
- **Accounting firms** — similar to consulting firms, but they also provide employee benefit audit services
- **Payroll providers** — new entrants that have targeted strategic relationships to provide a combination of the bundled and unbundled approach, while leveraging their payroll and database software management. They also play a key role in the day-to-day process of record keeping, as they track the deductions and provide them to the client for delivery to their record-keeping service provider

The following firms provide services to the recordkeepers or plan sponsors direct:

- **Attorneys** — creating the documents for the plans, ensuring qualified status, and cleaning up plans that are not in compliance
- **Plan document providers** — creating mass-produced plan documents, which many attorneys use
- **Record-keeping software providers** — the firms that provide the systems for the record-keeping service providers and TPA's, including record-keeping systems, trust systems, and compliance software
- **Communication firms** — As indicated, they provide communication materials and technology to record-keeping service providers or directly to the plan.
- **Directed Trustees/Clearing Firms** – Firms that provide mutual fund trading, separately managed pricing, produce trustee annual trustee reports, etc, for the recordkeepers.
- **Niche consulting firms** — they provide the service industry with their expertise

Several firms have exited the recordkeeping administration business, but have transitioned to profitable sectors of investment management or consulting.

The Service Models

Record-Keeping Service Providers

Record-Keeping Service Providers (RSPs) are firms that provide over 80% of the key services related to the plan, including:

- Facilitating flow of monies in and out of the plan and managing the activities of Directed Trustees (see below, but it is the firm that clears the mutual fund trades for the record keepers).

- Providing participant communications, including all record-keeping data, answering inquiries, as well as providing information to the participant to facilitate retirement planning and make ongoing deferral and investment decisions.

- Assembling a menu of investments from which the participants can make selections. This is the key element to the participant's success because participants are limited solely to this investment menu. If the funds selected do not meet prudent standards, the record-keeping service provider, investment advisor, and/or consultant may get fired and face future litigation for not performing their duties appropriately.

- Handling compliance/legal issues regarding plan design, government reporting, testing, and general consulting.

The two types of RSPs are:

1. **Closed-Architecture Service Providers** — Previously referred to as bundled providers, these firms provide one-stop shopping for all the five necessary services mentioned previously, with an emphasis on their own investment package as their core service and profit generator. Typically these are banks, mutual-fund companies and insurance companies. These firms do not need an outside-directed trustee to clear trades, which becomes a key factor in pricing and servicing the plan.

2. **Open-Architecture Service Providers** — Previously referred to as unbundled providers, an open-architecture firm generally provides one or two of the five necessary services mentioned previously. Unbundled providers traditionally place an emphasis on their record-keeping administration, com-

pliance, and consulting. Unbundled service providers tout their ability to quarterback the entire process and emphasize their flexibility in plan design and unlimited investment selections. The small-plan marketplace (serving companies with fewer than 500 employees) is generally served by the unbundled providers, of which there are over 3,000.

NOTE: *Both types of record keepers — open-architecture and closed architecture — are starting to look similar. In fact, the bundled strategy has transformed into more flexibility offering outside funds, and some of the unbundled firms have started to limit the number of funds they offer to clients. The open-architecture firms will and can work with other strategic partners to provide greater flexibility in services to the plan sponsor and participant.*

Plan sponsors or other parties retain record-keeping service providers through one of the following methods:

1. **Direct Model** — The record-keeping service provider is retained directly by the plan sponsor. This is the best way for controlling service expectations and maintaining a long relationship.

2. **Preferred-Provider Model** — The record-keeping service provider is hired through an investment advisor or broker, who owns the relationship; however, the record-keeping service provider still works directly with the plan sponsor. This approach is often used to eliminate any advisor responsibility related to the record-keeping service. It is important that the service provider be committed to serving the plan participant, plan sponsor, and investment advisor, in that order of priority. The key to success in this model is to make all of your clients look good.

Back-Office or Service Bureau Model

A service provider acts as the back-office record-keeping administrator for their partner (mutual-fund company, broker/dealer, bank, insurance company, and/or wirehouse), and has no direct contact with the plan sponsor. This model is not as prevalent today, due to efficiency and accountability issues, since the service provider is not the primary point of contact with the plan sponsor and participants. If this model is going to work, the lead firm must act only in an account-management role, which is more in line with the Preferred Provider Model.

TPA (Third-Party Administrator) Model

The record-keeping service provider is generally retained through an investment advisor or broker, whereby one service provider (usually insurance firms and mutual-fund companies) performs day-to-day record-keeping administration, and the second (or TPA) performs all compliance work including testing, vesting calculations, required government filings, and calculation of all distributions and loans. This model is very prevalent in the small-plan marketplace.

The power of this relationship is twofold:
- The TPA acts as an auditor of the day-to-day record-keeping financials
- The compliance role is segregated from the record-keeping service provider, which allows each firm to work on its strength

The issues of this popular approach:
- Requires all providers to be on the same page operationally (very difficult)
- The annual reconciliation process is manual, although the downloads from the record-keeping service provider to the TPA are electronic
- The plan sponsor has multiple relationships, and often the TPA tries to act as the lead party and handles all inflow and outflow of transactions (acting as a middleperson for the payroll input process and always handles distribution requests)
- Even for models that are 100% efficient, the total cost is not as low as the traditional record-keeping model (record-keeping administrator direct with the client)

ASP (Application Service Provider) MODEL or the BPO (Business Process Model)

The ASP Model is another misused word by many in the recordkeeping industry. The ASP Model is not providing recordkeeping software to recordkeeping service providers and TPA's on a hosted basis (that is simply a hosting service). Nor is it a recordkeeper convincing other recordkeepers to use their platform and services in a back-office environment. The ASP Model often discussed in our industry is really a Business Process Model whereby the BPO serves the recordkeeping service providers and TPA's with all of the following services or via an ala carte menu:

- Recordkeeping Administration via an Open Architecture Platform (day to day processing)
- TPA Services
- Call Center Services — IVR, e-chat, and customer service representatives
- Recordkeeping Software (hosting)
- Integration of all systems to provide total benefit outsourcing
- On-demand reporting and data retrieval

For recordkeeping service providers, they can move all the above tasks to the ASP Model and retain their identity as the service provider. Alternatively, they can retain the compliance or TPA component, and use the recordkeeping software at the BPO or their own. Over the course of the next few years, the numbers of BPO's will increase (some of which may be the full service providers today) and the number of full service recordkeeping service providers will decrease.

TPA's will view the BPO model as an upgrade to the current TPA Model. The BPO Model will increase the number of TPA's.

A History of the Record-Keeping Service Business

In the last fifteen years, defined-contribution record-keeping administration has evolved rapidly with continuing pressure on service providers to provide plan sponsors additional and higher-quality services for lower fees.

Late '70s, Early '80s

These were the days of very little compliance and no record-keeping systems. Money Purchase Pension Plans were the *en vogue* plan. Most of the administration work was performed by banks, insurance companies, actuaries, or by the company themselves. PCs and mainframes were nowhere to be found. Trust systems were used to hold the plan assets, and the good old-fashioned paper and pencil were used to perform participant breakdowns. Most plans hired an investment manager to manage one fund for the entire plan (participants did not have investment choices, nor were they clamoring for more funds).

The early 1980s was the start of the bundled service provider, as banks and insurance companies quickly realized they could provide basic record keeping and investment choices for their clients. The actuarial firms (all of the major consulting firms now) were essentially handed defined-contribution plans to administer, as they were already performing all of the services on the defined-benefit plan. This was the birth of the unbundled provider. The major regional and national banks provided discretionary trustee services to defined-contribution plans of all sizes, back in the days of trust fees as high as 50 basis points.

Separately managed funds and collective funds were the norm, as mutual funds were virtually non-existent. The fees for investment management for defined-contribution and defined-benefit plans were better than in today's environment, and, in fact, were based on graduating schedules. This was the tail end of companies creating defined-benefit plans as their emphasis for retirement benefits.

Mid and Late 1980s

In the early years of 401(k) plans, insurance firms and banks dominated the industry, with consulting firms trailing a distant third (however capturing a significant market share in the Fortune 500 marketplace). The revolution of the 401(k) legislation provided impetus for companies to focus retirement benefits on defined-contribution plans.

The workforce was becoming more mobile with less of a desire to stay with one company for their entire working career. Individuals were willing to give up their defined-benefit plan, even if they did understand it. The workforce wanted something they could put their hands on, that was portable. Instead of a person receiving a defined-benefit projection, they could now see something on paper, a participant statement or certificate.

Plans were updated annually, or quarterly, with some plans even going to a quicker monthly turnaround time. Many did not want this, due to the time and expense, and also because retirement plans should not be a monthly decision.

The banks were at the tail end of charging trustee or custodian fees that ranged anywhere from 10-100 basis points. What a great moneymaker for just holding the assets in a non-daily environment!

Compliance became a focus and a major reason plan sponsors started to outsource their record keeping. In the mid-1980s there were probably over 500 record-keeping systems and methods performed on Wangs and IBMs in a mainframe environment (back in the days when you had to submit your job, wait in queue for your tape to be posted, and then watch your job run). The mid-1980s was the period when the record-keeping software companies made their run, and many firms entering the record-keeping administration decided to use one of 15-20 available systems. Those of you who have been in this industry for a while will remember the pre-TEFRA compliance testing methodology, which was simply a 1/3 versus 2/3 comparison of net contributions, divided by net compensation (highly compensated versus non-highly compensated).

In the late 1980s, Fidelity started a marketing campaign that trivialized record-keeping administration, and placed an emphasis on participant communications and investments. Not only did they market these services, they executed their business plan and the birth of the daily valuation plan. The banks, insurance companies, and separate account managers started to lose their market share to Fidelity, and other mutual-fund bundled providers, due to poor investment performance, record-keeping administration, and participant communications. In addition, quarterly statements delivered 60 days after quarter-end to participants were no longer competitive in the marketplace. The new breed of service providers offered a higher level of service, including interactive voice response systems and daily valuation services as standard features.

The late 1980s also brought a new breed of sales to the marketplace, the investment advisor and broker. Many of the traditional record-keeping-only firms, for the first time, were facing the risk of losing their clients, and their fantastic profits. Consulting firms and record keepers were not charging by the participant back then, but were learning quickly that their business, built by actuaries, needed to change in order to stay competitive.

The mutual fund companies, dominated by Fidelity, and their bundled service offerings were leading the marketplace. The insurance companies were adapting quickly, but the banks were lagging, not only in their discretionary and clearing services, but their bundled products. The marketplace simply indicated bank investment management skills as too conservative. This period also marked the end of the high rate Guaranteed Insurance Contracts (GICs — as high as 18% guaranteed), as well as the introduction of some failed GICs, as interest rates plummeted.

The GIC marketplace quickly changed to a pooled fund approach (diversifying what many plan sponsors and participants took for granted as the safest investment), thus reducing the risk of holding one GIC contract within the plan. In addition, the managers of GICs changed their name to Stable-Value Funds, eliminating the word guarantee (as the marketplace found out that in the failed GICs, the only thing that was guaranteed was the interest, but the principal could be lost).

In my opinion, this was the end of a good era in investment-management pricing (with the exception of a few low-cost mutual fund companies). The banks, insurance companies, and the separate account managers that used collective-investment funds, or separately managed funds, were wiped out in one fell swoop with mutual funds. Investment management fees skyrocketed, all for convenience and to pay for the hefty marketing and sales fees.

The Early 1990s

Consulting firms and independents countered the bundled players with improved record-keeping services, appropriately labeled by the marketplace as 'unbundled,' with the help of mutual trading platform firms such as Charles Schwab (the first true directed trustee). With the introduction of Section 404(c), plan sponsors were encouraged to add funds. The unbundled firms' marketing campaigns were compelling, as the plan sponsor could hire the best record keeper, investment manager, trustee, and communication approach all coordinated under one umbrella, hence placing a premium on flexibility.

In a relatively young industry, virtually every financial service sector wanted to play in the marketplace, creating a large group of service providers performing record-keeping administration only (consulting firms, accounting firms, regional insurance firms, and independents), labeled as 'Record-Keeping-Only' firms. These record keepers required a platform to trade their clients' mutual funds and other investment vehicles, as their expertise was record keeping (or so they marketed, whether it was a low-cost solution or a premium service solution). Charles Schwab actively marketed the 'Record-Keeping-Only' firms, as the traditional banks fought to transition their practices to be clearing based (with lower fees and more investment-fund flexibility).

However, during the wild growth years of the 401(k) plan, many unbundled providers found out that providing daily valuation service was expensive, and, in most cases, losing money. In this period, unbundled record keepers were processing daily valuation in the most archaic forms:

- Daily trades faxed to the directed trustee or directly to the mutual fund (or worse yet, a broker)
- Most participant transfers across mutual-fund families were performed as sell Day 1, and then buy on Day 3, 4, or 5, whenever the sale settled
- Some record keepers were still accepting participating transfers via paper

The daily processing was performed the next day; therefore participants were generally a day lagging.

In a nutshell, a high percentage of plans were not 100% reconciled, and posting dividends was a living hell. If mutual fund dividends were posted within three months of the actual dividend, it was a major achievement.

This was the boom period for defined-contribution technology, especially the integration of record-keeping systems with voice response systems, as plan sponsors were demanding record-keeping service providers handle participant 401(k) questions directly. This integration with voice response technology was the best thing to happen to record-keeping service providers, as it allowed the elimination of paper transfer forms and countless write-offs for incorrectly keyed-in forms or forgotten transfers.

Prior to voice response systems, record keepers also took the brunt of the phantom transfer or election forms that were never sent in. This is not to say that record keepers never make mistakes; but one can certainly be suspicious when a participant complains two years later that their investment election was supposed to be in an equity fund, as opposed to the default money-market fund. In some cases, the equity fund would be down for the first nine months, but skyrocket in the next 15. Where were they in the 10th month? This also was the impetus for the first service contracts that outlined that all errors had to be reported within 30 or 90 days. With interactive voice response, you could simply demand that clients not use paper, because the write-off or risk was not worth it. The biggest question, back then, was how to handle a trade when the person did not have a touch-tone phone (of course 99% of America was covered). This might sound similar to some who proclaim the Internet will not work because their staff does not have access to a computer.

The Mid 1990s

The unbundled service providers started to get wiser as they realized that the daily valuation arena was no longer profitable, and the real profit margins in the business were derived primarily in the following areas:

- Any segment of the investment component
- Consulting and compliance (including legal)
- Traditional record keeping — Commonly known as balance forward

At this time, daily valuation was a must to retain clients and win new ones. In fact, most of the firms were using their daily valuation practices or business units as a loss-leader, in order to retain, or win, other business from their clients. For investment companies, it was to manage the money; for accounting and consulting firms, it was access to more lucrative consulting or audit engagements.

Due to the pressures of poor or no-profit margins, write-offs due to processing errors and high turnover in personnel, firms started to drop their record-keeping administration or sell their practices. The unbundled firms that stayed in the game started to leverage the mutual-fund industry through shareholder service fees and, sub-TAs, etc. These are forms of revenue sharing that are paid directly from the mutual fund to the record keeper, and will be discussed in Chapter II.

During the long "bull" run in the stock market, plan sponsors (and their brokers or advisors) focused on the record keeping/compliance portion of their plans, which only magnified the pressures record keepers were feeling. The two common reasons plan sponsors changed service providers in this period were poor record-keeping administration, and fees. The pressure of quality delivery, pricing, and lack of profitability, especially those tied to consulting and accounting firms, forced record keepers to shorten their long-term business plans for improving service, capabilities, and profit margins.

One of the key solutions for record-keeping service providers to again become profitable was the transition to Same Day/Late Day processing, thus eliminating carryover reconciliations each day (tracking buys and sells on separate days), a people-intensive process. Same day/late day processing reduces operation flow by 30-50%, hence simply shifting a plan to this approach will allow the record-keeping service provider to become more profitable, if their fees remain constant.

The same day/late day process was pushed by the mutual fund and record-keeping service provider to set technology and trading standards. This was the creation of the NSCC as a not-for-profit subsidiary of the DTC (Depository Trust Company) to settle all equity transactions on Wall Street.

A new breed of 'Directed Trustees' moved quickly to capture the new clearing platform and the market need from the record-keeping service providers. The traditional banks shied away from investing major dollars in an industry where they continued to lose market share and profit margins.

The major consulting firms started to focus on serving the large marketplace, and started to build their practice around total-benefits outsourcing.

Late 1990s

As the late 1990s approached, a new group of service providers emerged to serve the record keepers that wanted to provide their clients (plan sponsors) flexibility in fund selection and maximize their revenue sharing possibilities (regardless if brokers were involved). This new group, labeled 'Directed Trustees,' provided record keepers seamless links to clear mutual fund trades and cut checks for the plan sponsors in a cost-effective manner. In a nutshell, they were serving the market Charles Schwab could not, as well as taking a good piece of its business.

Today

Regardless of the service approach, plan sponsors are placing an emphasis on the following services:

- On-demand retirement modeling and asset -allocation tools for the plan participant
- Internet solutions at the participant and plan-sponsor level that continue to evolve with the latest in technology
- Individual participant advice
- Seeking a consultant or advisor that will help them with all of their important decisions (service provider, investment selection, plan design, etc.)
- A one-stop or integrated approach for all Employee Benefit services including health & welfare, that allow the employee to go to one site for all benefit questions and transactions

- Low fees
- An investment menu with depth and breadth

Record-keeping service providers of any size can serve companies of any size. From a plan-sponsor perspective, the service providers divided the plan sponsors into three segments:

- **Large-Market Plans** — Over 10,000 employees. Less than 20 firms compete for this space.
- **Middle Market** — Generally plans with assets above $3 million and over 3,000 record keepers fight for this business, not to mention all of the attorneys, brokers, advisors, consultants, etc. These are the plums for the record keepers, as it is possible to generate a profit in this marketplace, as the assets are large enough.
- **Small-Market Plan** — These are the small companies that most of the 3,000 record keepers will target, but most of the market-share leaders shy away from (or price so high as to not to make it attractive)

The evolution as of today:

- Software companies have dwindled to less than 5.
- Today, no one company is recognized as a quality leader.
- Record-keeping firms continue to pop up almost at the same rate as they are aggregating.
- Emphasis is on providing service to the participant, not the plan sponsor.
- The majority of plans with less than $3 million in assets are sold through brokers and investment advisors.
- The last five years has seen record keepers who held onto their 'sacred cow approach' fade away.
- Most of the record keepers use brokers and advisors to perform their sales function.
- Record keepers are continuing to leverage outside firms such as directed trustees and mutual-fund managers.
- Directed trustees are aggressively targeting the open-architecture firms.

A History of the Trustees of Defined-Contribution Assets

First, a brief review of the terms, before embarking on the history of the trustee/bank.

Discretionary Trustee — A bank or trust company that takes full fiduciary responsibility for the investments offered to the plan and how they are communicated to the participants. Plan-design responsibility is included only to the extent that it relates to how it affects the participants' selecting and changing funds. A discretionary trustee is nearly extinct today, due to our litigious society, but you can still find them at a hefty price. If you think you have a bank acting as a discretionary trustee, look at your contract closely.

Directed Trustee — Typically a bank or trust company that serves as a custodian of the plan's assets and performs all monetary transactions. Most directed trustees today are state chartered. Liability is limited to errors related to accurate and timely trades. The reason they are called 'directed trustees' is because they take all direction from the record-keeping service provider and are not responsible for any investment decisions on behalf of the plan or participant.

The optimal directed-trustee partner provides all of the following services at 100% quality levels and competitive pricing:

- Same Day/Late Day capabilities with a large mutual-fund universe (commonly referred to as NSCC capabilities, which means they can trade across two different fund families using that day's closing price.) From a participant's perspective, this means if you have same day/late day trading (which is the most efficient process), and you get your transfer request in before the market closes, your trades will happen at that day's closing price across all fund families.
- Linking between the two firms that is reliable from a quality and time perspective, maximizing the latest in technology (optimal partners provide information in the record keeper's format)
- Tracking and collecting revenue sharing for all types (the record-keeping service providers have difficulty keeping up with the latest maximum revenue sharing available through sub-TA's, platform fees, 12b-1's, dealers concessions, shareholder service fees, and marketing fees)

- Timely and accurate check-cutting, complete with state and national reporting through the 1099R process
- On-demand reporting (transaction and held positions)
- Long-term dedication to this line of business

Areas of concern as dictated by record-keeping administrators in relation to the 'directed trustee' service providers are:

- Lack of revenue sharing payment system or the negotiated sub-TA's are lower than other competitors (we will provide an inside look at the definitions related to defined-contribution investments in the next few chapters).
- Inadequate at state tax withholding. In fact, some firms decline to perform this function due to state charter (which is an excuse for not being able to perform the task).
- No seamless online brokerage option (commonly known as Individually Directed Accounts (IDAs))
- Comprehensive and reliable online reporting

Plan Trustee — People at the plan-sponsor company, or hired by the company, to act as a fiduciary on behalf of the plan. This is the group that has the most liability and requires the necessary bonding. Companies that think they have outsourced this function should review their contracts closely, as the trustee often has indemnified itself for virtually all plan issues.

The History

From a historical perspective, the top trustees in the defined-contribution marketplace in 1986 were virtually all of the national banks. Their service lines were simple:

- Holding assets for all defined-contribution plans
- Offering bundled services, including their investment approaches (not all of them)

By the end of the 1980s, these banks were facing increasing pressure to perform more services for far lower fees. They drastically lowered their fees as new players entered the industry — not only other banks, but also a far different player, a brokerage firm named Charles Schwab. Not only were the traditional banking powers lowering their fees and losing business to competitors, they were losing a significant portion of their revenues generated through their proprietary CIFs to the mutual-fund providers (see the history of record keepers above, as Fidelity had a major impact on the record-keeping service providers, as well as the banks). Plan sponsors wanted mutual funds, only, and the banks were no longer the key influencers with the plan sponsor. In 1992, Charles Schwab aggressively entered the marketplace to serve the directed-trustee function for the middle and large-plan marketplace, targeting the record-keeping service provider for new business. In fewer than six years, the traditional banks faced:

- Increased competition from more providers
- Lower directed-trustee fees
- Lost revenue from their investment-management services
- Increased costs to transition their platforms to a more clearing-based service that can trade more mutual-fund families on a daily basis (as opposed to less frequently since most plans were updated monthly or quarterly in the past; hence, participants were limited to making investment decisions monthly or quarterly)

In a nutshell, Charles Schwab offered a more seamless service, increased fund flexibility, and better fees. Charles Schwab was the first to target the record keeper.

Transition from Discretionary Trustee to Directed Trustee

The other major change for the bank powers has been the transition from discretionary trustee to directed trustee. This was a sound strategic move from a legal standpoint, because the discretionary trustee was responsible for everything related to the plan, while the directed trustee was only responsible for processing trades and checks in an accurate and timely manner. The downside to this strategy was that the traditional banks could no longer market their services as an additional insurance policy related to administration or fiduciary issues/errors.

Directed trustees became prevalent as they saw the need to help the record-keeping service providers with same day/late day trading (described previously). The new breed were smaller state-chartered banks or clearing entities that could move quickly (Security Trust, TRUSTlynx, Matrix, Circle Trust, Reliance, Sungaard Expiditor, and MidAtlantic).

41

Charles Schwab's strategy eliminated the traditional bank's power in the defined-contribution sector, as they lost a key component for success with the plan sponsor, which was controlling the client relationship. The traditional banks have lost significant revenues as trustee fees (basis points and transaction fees) plummeted from 1986-1996, as well as control of many of the investment offerings, since the plan sponsor was looking at the record-keeping service provider or advisor as the key influencer for investment-fund selection and directed-trustee decisions. In other words, the new 'Directed Trustee' was a service provider for the record keeper first, and the plan sponsor, second. These trends have caused the traditional players to exit the game or change their service offerings, and have spawned a whole new generation of trustees from smaller and more nimble firms that build their business around 'Directed Trustee' services.

Traditional national bank powers in the early 1990s aligned themselves with the large consulting firms to provide trustee services for their alliance funds in the Fortune 1000 marketplace. With the exception of a few, the others continued to build their bundled practices. Ironically, the number of national banks that entered the marketplace in the late 1980s was less than the number of firms that exited the business by 1995. A majority of these firms still continue to serve the defined-benefits sector, as it does not require mutual-fund trading daily, but more sophisticated services, such as trading for separately managed funds and foreign securities.

By 1998, a majority of the unbundled record-keeping service providers controlled the selection of the directed trustee, as opposed to 1980-1996 where the plan sponsor selected the directed trustee. The competition for the Record-Keeping-Only business in 2002 has essentially shrunk to less than 20 firms, with Charles Schwab and Fidelity leading the way, followed by four or five independent directed trustees. Fidelity, and all the remaining directed trustees, entered the marketplace after 1997.

Charles Schwab was essentially a lone player, targeting the record-keeping service providers for five years, and was working with over half of the unbundled record-keeping service providers by 1997. That year, the directed trustees, as we know them today, aggressively targeted the unbundled record-keeping service provider. Fidelity matched Charles Schwab's strategy, and the others targeted Charles Schwab's and Fidelity's weaknesses, which were broker-won business (commission business) and their inability to pay full revenue sharing to their record-keeping service providers' clients. The directed trustee marketplace is broken up into two camps — Fidelity and Schwab — and the other group consisting of Matrix, Security Trust, Reliance, MidAtlantic, and TRUSTlynx (just to name a few).

Today

When a record-keeping service provider is reviewing directed trustees in order to move business or award new business, they will review four components:

1. Price charged to plan sponsor (generally basis points on all assets in the plan)
2. Revenue sharing paid from mutual funds to the record-keeping service providers
3. Investment advisor/broker friendly
4. Technology (reducing the time spent by the record keeper in the process)

The directed-trustee business is a commodity business, and the winners are the ones that will best leverage revenue sharing from the mutual-fund families to payback to the record-keeping service providers, and also have an efficient technology approach.

CHAPTER II

Are Service Providers Benefiting More Than Plan Participants?

The participant is your client. Sometimes we forget this. It's only my opinion, but hiding the fees to win business means the participant ends up paying, and, in the long run, those that hide the fees will lose.

Hidden Fees

When fees are hidden, the participant usually pays more in investment-management expenses through a mutual-fund expense and/or a wrap fee. One of the easiest ways to show how the defined-contribution plan participant may be paying more than the person on the street is to look up a mutual-fund family on the Internet. Most mutual funds have multiple class share funds, or categories, for the same fund. The key difference is the investment expense ratio (and compensation to a broker). Determine which share class you have in your plan, and then compare it to the other funds. Most defined-contribution plan participants will be surprised to find they are not in the lowest expense ratio class, and hence, paying more.

To be fair, it is confusing; but as a rule, when somebody tells you "it's free," don't believe it. Check it out and you'll find that someone is paying for it. As nearly as I can tell, nothing is free in the securities industry.

In the mid-1980s, the sponsor paid for everything. Today, the participant seems to be paying for everything. In fact, we believe that plan sponsors, who are looking solely to save out-of-pocket costs, are really not performing their fiduciary role. They may save $2,000, while the participants end up paying $50,000 a year in extra fund fees. And that can come back to haunt you!

Here is the big eye opener: Anyone who gets paid for recommending a platform, or a certain number of mutual funds, is a *fiduciary* — whether they think so or not. When you opt for the so-called "hidden" fee, you're limiting the fund selection for the plan participants — unless you're exposing exactly what you're getting paid, as well as the information that participants can get the same funds for less, anywhere.

It would help if we all understood how anyone selling to the plan sponsor makes money:

Record keepers generate revenue from plans in two ways.
1. **Charging fees**, such as per-participant fees, base fees, asset-based fees and transaction fees
2. **Revenue received from mutual-fund companies** (non-commission through Sub-TAs, or shareholder service fees as described below)

Clients can either charge the record-keeping fees to the plan (participants pay it) or pay for it out-of-pocket. The record-keeping service providers have the option of disclosing any revenue received from mutual fund companies as an offset to the fee, or they can build the anticipated revenue into their fee quote.

Revenue directly received from mutual funds is what we call Sub-TA fees (Sub-Transfer fees). The mutual funds will pay these fees because they only have to track one account on their system (the plan name, which could have 5,000 participants), and not one account for each participant, as this is what the record keeper is doing. They're willing to give up part of their investment-management fee for that, so they don't have to track 5,000 accounts.

Sub-transfer fees are generally paid only to record keepers, but one can say that these fees are more like marketing incentives from the mutual fund companies, as opposed to an operational efficiency incentive. If it were simply an operational incentive, all the mutual funds would have roughly the same incentive amount — that being what the mutual funds pay a transfer agent, whether it's a directed trustee or record keeper.

There is an actual *marketing fee* that may be paid for prominent placement on the investment menu served to plan sponsors or brokers. These marketing fees have traditionally been paid to broker/dealers to "push" their funds, and that's why you may see brokers recommending certain funds over others. In fact, these fees can be extended to certain record keepers, if they so negotiate, in what we typically call enhanced revenue sharing. That marketing fee is not paid out of the investment expense of the mutual fund; it's paid from the mutual-fund company. This can be as high as 25 basis points, but is normally around 10 to 15 basis points.

To better serve the record-keeping service providers, "enhanced revenue sharing" recapture firms are now sprouting up to help them maximize their revenue from mutual-fund companies. The more assets these firms have, the better they can negotiate. In addition, the best time to target the mutual funds is when fund performance is down, and they are concerned with retaining assets.

As a side note, with all of the firms asking the mutual-fund companies to pay more in the retirement service sector, some mutual-fund companies are putting minimums on their IRA rollovers and 401(k) plans. They are doing this because they don't want to have a lot of small accounts and have to pay so much in revenue sharing that they're losing money.

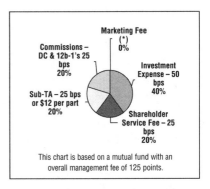

This chart is based on a mutual fund with an overall management fee of 125 points.

A mutual fund makes money, very simply, by its investment expense.

However, most of the mutual funds have now caught onto a game where they're willing to pay something more to brokers, record keepers, and clearing firms. The result is adding another share class that adds to the overall investment expense.

Investment advisors are typically fee-for-service.

Pretty simple. They will charge a fully disclosed, asset-based fee for their services. On the other hand, a broker/registered representative is compensated via commissions. As a registered representative or investment advisor, you cannot charge an asset-based fee and also receive commissions (although you could probably still find a few). Commission-only brokers do not necessarily disclose their commissions (although we think they should). Our favorite approach is that of investment advisors who use any commissions to offset their fees, otherwise known as the "Full Disclosure Model." We also prefer brokers who use a part of their commissions to offset plan-sponsor expenses, such as record-keeping administration.

Directed trustees will charge an asset-based fee at the plan level.
Now, as discussed in the first chapter, the record keeper pays for most of these fees so they can charge a pseudo-bundled fee to the plan sponsor. However, directed trustees make a lot of money on float, and float is basically from outgoing distribution checks.

When a participant leaves a plan, those monies are moved out of the plan and held in a holding account where the trustee is making money on the interest. On average, it takes about one week for the participant to cash a check. Back in the old days, we were told to mail checks on Thursday, so we could get more float on the weekend. You wouldn't want to send them on a Monday because they would be cashed by the end of the week. That made more sense ten or fifteen years ago, because mail delivery was slower, but now the mail generally arrives within a day or two.

Directed trustees also make money on shareholder-service fees. Similar to Sub-TA fees, the mutual fund will pay the directed trustee or the clearing firm anywhere from five to 25 basis points. That's almost as much as a Sub-TA. Some funds pay both. Some will pay both up to a certain amount; after that, you have to fight for more. Record-keeping service providers have done an excellent job of negotiating with their directed trustee fees to include a percentage of the shareholder-service fees as a rebate.

Finally, some directed trustees will require plans to insert their money market funds in order to provide recordkeeping service providers a lower asset based fee. This is especially true in providing a fee competitive solution in the small plan marketplace.

Insurance Companies.
The insurance companies use wrappers, or sometimes build it into the so-called group annuity contract. If you are using a group annuity contract you are not

investing directly into mutual funds, as many think they are. Group annuity contracts are insurance contracts, so you invest in sub-accounts, not mutual funds. The sub-accounts invest in the mutual funds; so, essentially, you' re getting a mutual fund with an extra layer of fees. Unlike mutual funds, where an investor buys shares, in group- annuity contracts, participants receive units of the sub-account. The insurance companies then build additional fees into the unit value so it is very difficult to determine the actual fees. Essentially, via the sub-account, they are taking the mutual fund and building an additional fee at the expense of the plan participant. That fee could be as high as 150 basis points!

A lot of insurance companies work with fee-for-service advisors, which is added onto the group annuity fee. For the contract-averse readers, it can take about two weeks to figure out what they're doing, as it is rarely disclosed in an easy-to-read format. We could start a business just reading insurance contracts to find out what they're really charging, and what the surrender charges are.

We hate to see the hidden surrender charges. The participant sees no costs up front, including no up-front fees for investing in the sub-accounts; then suddenly, the plan decides to switch record-keeping service providers and is staring at a surrender charge as high as seven percent. And every year, in which the participant puts in new monies, the seven-year clock starts ticking anew — a perpetual loop you can't escape. Today, there are still surrender fees in some group annuity contracts, but many insurance carriers are moving away from this approach, OR provide other pricing solutions to avoid having surrender fees in the contract. In all fairness to the insurance companies, they *are* getting better.

Some mutual funds also have surrender fees (Share Class B and/or C), typically in the small-plan marketplace with less than $250,000 in plan assets. The surrender fee allows them to recover the commissions they have paid to the broker and may cover their record-keeping expense, so there's a reason for putting it in place, even though some of the costs are prohibitive. In terms of record-keeping expense, it would almost be better for the plan sponsor to pay the cost out-of-pocket. For the broker, recommending a different share class, such as Class A with front-end loads waived, is the best solution. In the past, it was difficult to use A-share class funds in the small marketplace because of the up-front loads. In today's marketplace, there are platforms, which allow even new plans without any assets, access to A-share class funds at Net Asset Value (NAV).

Who's really benefiting from all this? Certainly not the participant. Generally, it's those service providers in the investment side of the equation. Remember, nobody does anything for free, however as a consumer, isn't full disclosure the most desirable approach?

Bad Fees to Watch Out For

- **Up-front loads in small plans** — That's just a loaded mutual fund. Cost-wise that could be higher than five percent.

- **Back-end or surrender fees** — These are often called CDSCs (contingent deferred sales charges). With some surrender fees, you can never move the plan without paying a fee, upwards of five to seven percent.

- **High expense ratio funds** — Know the share class you are buying, as well as the alternatives, as you may have access to a lower investment expense ratio, which will benefit the plan participant.

  Rarely will anyone ask the question: What's the lowest expense ratio I can get for the participant? In fact, some industry insiders will ask: What are the funds that will pay me the most? Very few people think of the participant first, but this has to change.

  There's a reason Vanguard and hosts of independent record keepers do well—because they have lower expense ratio funds. That's their whole premise. They don't have multiple client shares and they don't pay brokers. They state: "Our fees are our fees." Some may think their record-keeping fees are high, but as a whole, they're really not.

- **"All-inclusive"** — This is one of the worst ones, in my opinion. You'll see record keepers, whether open architecture or closed architecture, say, "Everything's included." Yes, it's included, but six to nine months later, a compliance test costs $3000. Or, when you have to resubmit your payroll data, you find you're charged for it. Little stuff just comes out of the woodwork.

  Many consulting firms will bid a plan on a pure participant count or base fee, as opposed to an asset-based fee. However, increases in fees tend to work their way up every year. The first year might be five to ten percent, and within three or four years, it's not uncommon for the fees to be 50 to 75 percent higher. Rarely have I seen them go down. In actuality, the only way to get your fees to go down is to put your plan out to bid. Oftentimes, the service provider will re-bid much lower than what the plan sponsor is currently paying, with obvious consequences.

When I consult with record keepers or directed trustees, I caution them to review the fees they are charging their clients. If their fees are higher for an existing client than what they would bid out for a similar plan, they'd better review their fee schedule to make sure it is right, or that their client is receiving more services.

- **Loan fees** — Many firms are stuck in an old-school mentality. They don't change their process even though it may be costing 20 percent more than a newer process, and the client may not even care about it (quarterly paper participant statements are a recent example). Loan fees are the reverse issue, where a high fee was put in place many years ago as a deterrent to participants taking loans, because they were such a pain to process. The average loan fee would be $50 to $150 charged up front, with a recurring fee of $25 to $100 a year for the term of the loan, and would be added to the loan principal. Everybody was happy because the participant got their loan and the plan sponsor wasn't paying the fees. Now, it's all automated, so the excellent record keepers have lowered or eliminated these fees, or have used these fees to offset their standard record-keeping fees.

Loan fees should be nominal. With current technology, you just go into the system and you model the loan over the Internet and then you execute. The cost shouldn't be any more than $25 to cut the check. No longer is the plan sponsor involved (if you use the noteless loan process).

Another built-in deterrent is the interest being charged. For a small loan, the money may cost one or two points above prime, but the APR charged to the participant could be 20 or 25 percent, or even higher — because they're taking such a small loan and the fees are so high. I've seen $500 loans where the fees totaled $200!

What fees should be charged?

My beef isn't with the high expense-ratio funds, as long as the plan sponsor has an itemized list of all fees that are paid, and to whom. But should the participant really be paying most of the record-keeping fee? Record-keeping fees have been forced lower because companies have been asked to "sharpen their pencils," and also because investment managers are buying record-keeping businesses as a means of increasing assets.

What they really should be doing is taking the lower expense-ratio fund and then paying out of pocket, or charging the fees to the participant. Let's say a service provider needs $20,000 to cover their record-keeping costs. One way is to charge zero, and get the money through the mutual-fund companies and transaction fees, such as loan fees, that are paid by the participant. So the mutual funds are simply creating a new class of share that makes sure the record keeper is getting their $20,000, without cutting into their revenues of the fund investment expense. The issue is that the participant is paying for this through a higher investment expense, and is most likely paying even more than the additional $20,000. And when you add a broker, the expense is even greater.

This could be resolved in one fell swoop by having the sponsor pay the record keeper's fee, or at least having the option of receiving an invoice before deciding what to do.

Just consider this scenario: Suppose an employee found out that over the years of their work career a couple of hundred-thousand dollars had been lost because of higher fees in the investment funds than the average mutual-fund fee. Would they have a case?

In court, the employee says: "Judge, I could have gotten that fund at 80 basis points, but instead I've had to pay 200 basis points. I'm paying 120 basis points more, for what?" The judge turns to the sponsor and asks: "Did you have to pay any fees?"

I'd rather have that participant see that fee come out quarter by quarter, and have to explain it to them, as opposed to it being hidden, only to be revealed years later in court. The plan sponsor is the one who takes the easy route and is just as guilty as all of us who are not disclosing fees in the service industry. *The fees might be on the high side, but as long as you tell your participant what they are for, then you, as the plan sponsor, can go to sleep at night.*

The record keepers have been beaten down on price so much by the brokers and the plan sponsor, that conversion fees have been eliminated — even though the record keeper will spend more time performing the conversion than they will during the first 12 months in the plan. Record keepers used to charge conversion fees anywhere from $2000 to $50,000 depending on the size of the plan. Now the marketplace doesn't accept conversion fees. So where do those fees come from? The mutual funds—at the expense of the participant.

I'm not saying all plan sponsors should take out all these fees. What I'm saying is that all the fees should be disclosed.

But there's also the argument that this is your company and these are benefits to you. By the plan sponsors paying these fees, pretax, they, in effect, increase the employees' benefits. At a minimum, the plan sponsor should be making sure all plan fees are appropriate, and that they understand the fees within the fees.

A recap of service fees

Possible service fees to the participant and/or plan sponsor are:

- **Record-Keeping Administration Fees**
- **Trustee or Clearing Fees**
- **Investment Management Fees** (the management expense in the mutual fund.) Watch out for the actual investment expenses for each fund, as they may be subsidizing all of the service providers at fees higher than deemed appropriate.
  - **Sub-TAs**
  - **Shareholder Service Fees**
  - **Commissions Paid by Mutual Funds**
    Dealer Concessions—Commission paid to brokers on all new monies, up-front sales charges (could be higher than 5%) or finders' fees (generally 1%)
    12b-1s—A recurring commission paid to the broker, typically 25 basis points, but can go as high as 100 basis points
  - **An Administrative 12b-1**—To clarify, a 12b-1 is a commission paid to brokers. But now I'm hearing that an administrative 12b-1 will go to a broker-dealer or a platform, but not the broker. The incentive is to get your brokerage to sell those funds.
  - **Marketing Fees**—We need to crack down on these fees, today, because they are not paid through any investment expense, and this is

where a lot of litigation is going to happen. Those that accept these fees and push these funds, whether they are good or bad, do not have the participants' best interests at heart. They have more incentive to sell funds that offer marketing fees than any others. For example, if I have 20 funds on my platform, and seven pay marketing fees, which am I inclined to recommend? The ones that pay the marketing fees, and I'm not disclosing that.

Marketing fees are prominent in broker-dealers; however, they're now starting to transition over to record keepers. Mutual funds have done a good job of saying: "You placed me prominently on your marketing materials, so I'm going to pay you these marketing fees." And it's called *enhanced revenue sharing*. But what does it really enhance? The pockets of those who sell plans!

- **Investment Advisory Fees** — Asset based fees charged on top of the investment management or mutual fund fees.

- **Group Annuity or Wrap Fees** — Asset based fees, similar to the investment advisory fees, but are charged by the platform for the right to use the platform. In some cases, a group annuity or wrap fee is an addition to the investment advisory fee.

Fee Analysis — or How to Compare Apples to Oranges

An understanding of the difference between an open architecture versus a closed-architecture provider is the first step to recognizing the true costs involved. Then you must be able to accurately compare the dollar cost difference, as well as the trade-offs for one solution over the other.

Closed-architecture service providers will have a limited fund menu, but will tell you that they have the appropriate fund for each asset class. An example of a closed-architecture provider is a mutual-fund company, or an insurance company and their group annuity solution. In contrast, open-architecture service providers do not have proprietary mutual funds, but will provide you the flexibility to select an investment menu from a wide array of investments, including mutual funds, money managers, collective funds, etc.

When selecting a closed-architecture provider, it is clear that investment management fees are used to subsidize record-keeping administration fees, which on the outside, allows them to appear very cost competitive. Along with the seamless integration between record keeping, investments and trustee services, it makes this approach very attractive.

What makes the open-architecture approach attractive? The ability to offer the best fund in each asset class as appropriate for the plan, with an emphasis on plan-design flexibility and compliance. In the past, closed architecture had an advantage with seamless integration of record keeping, investments and trustee services. Today, technology has allowed open-architecture providers to offer the same seamless integration, AND ability to leverage revenue sharing from the mutual-fund families, so they can be as competitive, or even more competitive, than closed-architecture firms.

When selecting the appropriate solution, it is important for your plan to determine what is most important for your participants (and obviously the company, from a compliance perspective). Before embarking on the various intricacies in the record keeping and communications areas, it is essential to understand the fee game played by both provider types.

Then, how *do* you compare fees between the providers and get a true 'apples-to-apples' comparison?

To reiterate, nothing is "free." Having said that, your plan may receive a very low record-keeping administration bid or have no fees at all, even if you don't have asset- buying power. How can these providers be profitable while providing a "free" or low-cost plan? Through technology, many service providers have streamlined the record-keeping administration process, and leveraged enough revenue sharing from the mutual-fund industry to almost completely offset the expense to administer a plan.

The next question is where is this revenue-sharing coming from, and how does it affect the plan and its participants? First, the most important rule of thumb when reviewing fees is to not focus on the record-keeping portion only, as many will offer a low-cost or free plan. Often plan sponsors look only at the record-keeping administration fee, as this is the fee they have to pay (although plans have the option of charging fees to the trust).

To put this in perspective, compare the following two record-keeping bids for a plan with $5 million in assets. Here are their respective bids, with the assumption that the services and investment portfolios are equal (60% in Equities and 40% in Fixed):

Annual Record-Keeping Fees

Service Provider A................................$10,000
Service Provider B................................$ 0

All services being equal, it seems like a no-brainer to select Service Provider B. However, lets compare their average investment expense:

Average Investment Expense   Annual Investment Expense

Service Provider A   75 basis points (.75%)............$37,500
Service Provider B   150 basis points (1.5%)...........$75,000

With the above information, the obvious choice is to select Service Provider A, as the participants would have .75% less in expenses each year, not including the compounding effect. In this straightforward example, the plan would be much better off if the record-keeping fees were charged against the plan, as the participants are still better off in the short and long term.

Obviously, the comparisons are more complex as each service provider will offer an array of funds. In order to compare the service providers on an "apples-to-apples" basis, you will need to have the funds selected during the review process. What really makes this difficult is that no one can predict the future return of any fund.

There is an old axiom in the industry: Any investor will pay a higher invest-ment-management fee when the performance is higher. Less subtly, an investor will pay an expense ratio of 1.5% for a fund with a history of 20% returns, as compared to 1% for a fund with a history of 10% returns (assuming the funds are in the same class). Before digressing too far, risk obviously plays a compo-nent; therefore, the longer the time horizon for comparison of funds, the better.

Back to the example above, Service Provider B was clearly subsidized from the investment funds for its record-keeping expense. Coming from the record keepers' perspective, what is really scary, is that approximately 70% - 90% of the work related to the plan is performed by the record keeper, yet in most cases the record keepers are the ones that have to sharpen the pencil in the bidding process. Simply stated, the record keeper does 70%-90% of the work, for a small percentage of the total fees associated with the plan. Obviously these percentages change, based on the size of the plan in terms of assets, but the ratio will be tilted heavily to the investment-fund expenses. This will be true for bundled or unbundled service providers.

In the past, closed-architecture service providers had a built-in advantage in bidding fees, as they could clearly bundle all services under one fee umbrella.

As mentioned, open-architecture providers also leverage the mutual-fund industry to competitively price their services. Record-keeping administrators provide a service, not only to the plan sponsor and plan participant, but also to the mutual-fund families. Record-keeping administrators track participant account information so fund families do not have to, and for this, some mutual-fund families will pay record-keeping service providers.

Who incurs these fees and how are they paid? Each mutual-fund family assigns an expense ratio to their funds. From this expense ratio, mutual funds pay many different entities, including fund managers, distribution partners, investment advisors, record-keeping administrators, etc. The following is a simplified example of revenue sharing from a fund family, assuming an expense ratio of 1.0%:

Investment Manager(s)	0.25%
Marketing/Distribution Fee	0.25%
12b-1 Fee	0.25%
Sub-TA Fee	0.10%
Shareholder Service Fee:	0.15%
TOTAL	1.00%

Please note: The above is for illustrative purposes only and each revenue-sharing component will differ, depending on fund family and share class of the mutual fund.

Using the above example, a mutual fund family that does not pay the broker a 12b-1 fee will have a lower expense ratio, as this fee does not have to be built into the fund's expense ratio.

As mentioned, mutual-fund families will pay record-keeping administrators for their services. Generally, these revenue-sharing components can come from shareholder service fees or Sub-TA fees, however they can pay 12b-1 fees to the recordkeeper if a broker or advisor is not involved. Most open-architecture firms pass back the revenue to the plan sponsor either in a direct or indirect offset. Direct offsets are the best answer, in order for the client to understand and know all of the fee arrangements.

The mutual funds have become very aggressive in their dealings with record keepers. There is more "revenue sharing" money available today than there was one year ago, as fund families recognize the major distribution channels through record keepers and trustees/custodians Fund families typically offer up to 25-50 basis points through 12b-1s, sub-accounting or sub-transfer agent fees, and shareholder service fees. Some funds even pay one-time finder's fees (ranging from 25-100 basis points).

The following chart provides an insight into the average total fees paid by plan sponsors.

THE COST OF PLAN SPONSORSHIP

Average Annual Total Plan Expenses

	Record-Keeping & Administration	Investment Fee	Trustee	Total Plan Expenses
100 Participants	$4,126	$47,005	$826	$51,957
1,000 Participants	$20,140	$448,850	$2,390	$471,380
5,000 Participants	$94,350	$2,203,750	$3,450	$2,301,550

Average Annual Total Expenses per Plan Participant

	Record-Keeping & Administration	Investment Fee	Trustee	Total Plan Expenses
100 Participants	$41.26	$470.05	$8.26	$519.57
1,000 Participants	$20.14	$448.85	$2.39	$471.38
5,000 Participants	$18.87	$440.75	$0.69	$460.31

Average Annual Total Plan Expenses as % of Plan Assets

	Record-Keeping & Administration	Investment Fee	Trustee	Total Plan Expenses
100 Participants	0.10%	1.18%	0.02%	1.30%
1,000 Participants	0.05%	1.12%	0.01%	1.18%
5,000 Participants	0.05%	1.10%	0.001%	1.15%

Are Service Providers Benefiting More Than Plan Participants?

Of all providers, it is most difficult to determine exact fees of insurance companies, especially in the group-annuity contracts. When comparing group-annuity contracts, be aware of the following:

- Participants are investing in sub-accounts not directly into mutual funds. More importantly, when providing performance data, they may be illustrating actual mutual-fund performance prior to being a sub-account within the group annuity, so performance will not include any wrap fees that would have been charged by the insurance company.
- Fixed Mortality and Expense Fees, regardless of plan size
- Wrap Fees
- Surrender Charge

CHAPTER III

The Value of a Trusted Consultant

To whom do you turn if your defined-contribution plan is not running efficiently, or your participants are not satisfied or, worse yet, are facing compliance issues? Your firm may already have trusted advisors such as your auditor, accountant, payroll provider, and HR systems; but are they unbiased? Several websites have popped up to provide you information as well. However, do any of these sites or advisors have any information that is deeper than marketing information, or that is not biased?

We are in an industry where our only watchdogs are the press, some specialized industry organizations, and those of us serving the industry. In my opinion, record-keeping service providers are members of one of the most honest professions in the world. Unfortunately, articles in mainstream papers such as *USA Today* are doing their best to alarm everyone by showcasing the less than one percent of companies who do not fund their retirement plans, or make poor decisions in plan design. If they only focused on our own government's Social Security plan, they could educate citizens on the many myths around Social Security. And, we might actually see true reform. That's one plan we are all part of, but the popular press refuses to address the issue honestly, other than saying we may run out of money.

Yet when the owner of a plan with 50 employees embezzles money, the popular press cries for major pension-plan reform. Just who is the embezzler on our Social Security fund? Is it technically any different when our government does not set aside the excess money each year, but instead uses it to pay its bills? We throw embezzlers in jail for being dishonest, and rightly so. All it takes is intellectual honesty and ethics when presenting issues, and people can make their own decisions.

In relation to hidden fees, it is the same ethics issue. If everyone discloses their revenues from the plans, the plan sponsors will be satisfying a good portion of their fiduciary responsibility. Your trusted advisor or consultant must disclose this as well. Whether you are a plan sponsor or a service provider in this industry, perform your due diligence, and don't just go with the first person you meet, or the consultant or advisor who says they can lower your fees. Don't forget, this is interpreted as lower out-of-pocket fees, and, most likely, higher overall fees to the plan participant.

If a previous advisor or consultant has burned you, don't turn to the Internet for a solution. There are a number of websites that proclaim they have inside information and that they are the one-stop shop for hiring service providers. In fact, many have tried to become one-stop shops and failed. The reason is that none of these websites have true rating systems, or actually perform their own qualitative research. The key to these websites is finding out who owns them, and how they make a profit. Once you find out this information, it is easier to find out if there is a bias. Interestingly enough, websites such as these often base their rating systems on marketing input and fees paid by the service providers they list. Until they can tell me that they have performed on-site visits to all of the record keepers in their listings, and that they can provide their interview and research criteria, these sites will be nothing more than aggregators of marketing information.

Search Consultants

Without the proper watchdogs, to whom do you turn? There are a plethora of consultants that design Request for Proposals (RFPs) and facilitate searches. But, what is the real value, when most of the answers are marketing responses? These searches can be on behalf of plan sponsors, or service providers seeking a partner, vendor, or simply hiring a consultant for strategy or operations efficiency. How do you know your consultant knows what he or she is talking about, when in this business, simply being able to pronounce ERISA, ERSA, and TRA can make one sound smart?

For starters, if you are seeking an expert in the industry, ask your trusted advisors about the top consultants in the area. Then, when you talk to those consultants, ask them who their competitors are, or who the best service providers in the business are (and then ask why). If they don't know who their competition is, or can't provide an in-depth answer on the service providers, then they probably don't know the service providers very well. This industry is not that big, and all of us in the industry know who is who—locally, regionally, and nationally.

Key Questions for Consultants

Once you have a list of three to five consultants, ask them the following five questions:

1. How many service providers have you visited and performed true due diligence on, without the benefit of being paid on another search (in the last year, or three years)? (*Mutual fund and investment managers visit companies they invest in, or are thinking about investing in. If the consultant is dedicated to this line of business, they will have that list. And don't fall for the line that they receive all the providers' literature, and meet with them in their offices or at professional conferences.*)

2. In what capacities have you served in the industry? Specifically, what services have you performed for the end clients—the participants—that make you an expert? (*Those that have performed record-keeping administration, participant communications, and been directed trustees have a good idea of what the customer is looking for.*)

3. How do you get paid? (*Will they put in writing that they are not receiving soft dollars from any of the service providers they are recommending? Furthermore, will they stipulate that they will not include their own company in the search process? Some would think that is common sense, but you would be surprised how many have played both sides of the fence.*)

4. What are the five most important questions you would ask a record-keeping service provider, if you were limited to five? (*This will cut through the garbage, and if participant communications, investments, service guarantees, and fiduciary responsibility do not come up, RUN.*)

5. How do you produce your comparison reports? Do you provide a rating and how do you come up with the rating? (*If it is based solely on the RFP and marketing materials, then it is only rating their marketing capabilities. If they use certain questions to derive the rating, make sure you know the questions, as there are*

some excellent ones. In relation to fees, do they break out all of the revenue-sharing components based on their research, or is it simply through their RFP?)

Bottom Line: *Find someone who is providing more information than standard marketing responses.*

The RFP process is tedious, so make sure you do not have your search consultant rack up fees for work you can be doing yourself, or work that is not needed. Consulting searches can range anywhere from $5,000 - $30,000 if you hire them to perform all functions.

The best consultants are probably busy; hence, if you hire them, make sure you know who is performing the actual work. It is easy to hire the big-name consultant, and then find later that most of the work is performed by someone else within the firm. Make sure to get a breakdown of the project with specifics on timing, and who is performing the work.

My advice is to perform as much of the work as possible internally, and use the consultants for the qualitative process, digging deep into the responses and on-site presentations. The latter is where consultants are the most valuable, as they can ask the tough questions for you.

Investment Advisors/Brokers

Similar to consultants, investment advisors and brokers should be hired on their ability to serve you. In review, there are two ways investment advisors and brokers get paid:

1. **Fee for Service** — An-asset based fee on all assets under management, that is added to the mutual-fund investment expenses. The average asset-based fee ranges from 50-225 basis points, depending on the size of the plan and complexity of the relationship. Most advisors offset any fund management commissions against their asset-based fee.

2. **Commissions** — Paid from the investment fund expense. A typical commission is 1 percent on all new assets, and 25 basis points on recurring assets.

At the onset, it might appear the commission is best; however, the major advantage of a fee-for-service advisor can be as follows:

- They actually pick the funds or narrow large menus down to acceptable funds
- They take on a co-fiduciary role
- The advisor fee is dynamic and may be lowered as assets grow

In our litigious society and volatile stock markets, a good investment advisor can prove invaluable. In the large-plan marketplace, the investment advisor is often only hired to perform manager searches, investment policy creation, and monitoring. The investment advisor's fee is typically much lower for the large-plan marketplace and is often a set fee, such as $50,000. In the small and middle marketplace, the investment advisor and broker are often responsible for selling the record-keeping administration solution.

Key Questions for Advisors/Brokers

The key service many investment advisors and brokers perform, outside of investment selection, is participant communications. The level of involvement is crucial to your success. Here are the questions you should ask of your prospective advisor or broker:

1. What revenues do you receive from the funds? Do you use any of these revenues to directly subsidize participant communications or record-keeping administration fees?

2. Does your contract stipulate that you are a co-fiduciary? If not, does the contract indicate the plan sponsor is ultimately responsible for selecting the investment menu? (*That is a red flag for you, as it indicates they take no responsibility for the investment selection, but they are getting compensated from it*).

3. What level of participant communications will you commit to? Will you present an annual participant communication plan?

4. Will you provide one-on-one advice at the participant level?

5. If involved in the sales process for a record-keeping service provider, what record keepers have you worked with and which ones are you currently working with? (*Ask how they select these record keepers.*)

The investment advisor or broker may be your most important ally in your plan; make sure they are providing you the level of service that is commensurate with their revenue.

CHAPTER IV

The Process of Selecting a Record-Keeping Service Provider

I f you are a plan sponsor searching for a new record-keeping service provider, it is crucial to understand your candidate's primary business plan to determine if record-keeping administration is a core business for the firm. Why? If it is not, then their long-term commitment to appropriately investing in people and technology in the future is at question. Make sure you are in control of the process, and do not allow the service providers to sell you a solution that fits their strengths and business goals, as opposed to your company and culture.

There are a number of accounting and consulting firms, banks, and mutual-fund companies that provide record-keeping administration as a means of garnering clients for another line of business, such as investment management, consulting, or audit/accounting services. Many of these firms are successful, but it is the record-keeping administration that may not live up to its company's profitability or quality goals. Hence, these financial service firms may look down on their own record-keeping administration group.

Comparing quality in record-keeping administration to investment management, or auditing, is not a fair comparison. Record-keeping administration, performed correctly, is not as easy as it looks, nor is it a low-cost venture. Unfortunately, being unjustly looked down upon by the rest of the firm puts a lot of stress on the record-keeping administration department, which can lead to lower overall performance, and ultimately, to lost clients.

Can this effect be reversed? Absolutely, but it must include the complete buy-in of the entire management team. It begins with having an environment that is comfortable with ever-changing technology. And although technology can provide an edge in winning business, the long-term strength of the best record-keeping service provider is its people. Training is a priority, and should include cross training the other business units to effect a broad understanding of the record-keeping service industry.

Bottom Line: *Make sure the record keeper you are hiring is one that is embraced by its parent company, if it is a part of a larger company. If the record keeper is an independent, make sure they have the financial stability, as well as the commitment to service and invest in their product.*

The Selection Process

The selection really boils down to the following four components:

1. Competitive fees
2. Cutting-edge technology (making all inquiry and transaction information readily available to the plan participants and plan sponsors)
3. Depth and breadth of the investment-fund selection
4. An effective participant communication campaign

Ideally, a plan sponsor should design the plan first, and then select the service provider through one of three methods:

1. A complete and exhaustive Request for Proposal (RFP) search
   - Identify who will receive the RFPs
   - Send the RFP with cover letter, plan information, key characteristics of the optimal service provider, and schedule
   - Review the RFPs
   - Select finalists
   - Finalist presentations
   - Conduct on-site visits
   - Service contract and fee negotiation phase

2. Ask your trusted advisors for recommendations and proceed with a modified process as above, beginning at the finalist presentations step
3. Use a search consultant

The RFP

With all the time spent by search consultants and organizations creating RFPs, they could have just as easily created an internal rating system using outside audits. Until our business adopts an ISO 9000 approach (an accrediting process used by the manufacturing sector that provides the buyers of suppliers products an accreditation that the suppliers meet certain standards, such as quality and standard process flow), service providers are limited only by integrity, regarding their capabilities and services.

In relation to RFP design, I have seen hundreds in my time, including the infamous SPARK proposal, written by industry experts, that was supposed to revolutionize the process and reduce search costs at the plan sponsor level. You can tell the rookies a mile away; they ask too many questions!

A sample RFP kit can be found in the Appendix, but here are some guidelines to follow using the RFP approach:

- Design your optimal plan before sending out an RFP or interviewing candidates.

- Do not send courtesy RFPs; they only waste everyone's time.

- Keep the RFP short and concise, eliminating questions that really do not tell you anything about the provider.

- Send a cover letter containing the RFP timeline and stick to it. It is better to build in extra time for each phase of the RFP, than to create false expectations.

- Give the candidates a complete history of your plan and your criteria for selecting a service provider (this can be highlighted in the cover letter). Include a copy of last year's Form 5500, plan document, SPD, and sample participant communications.

- Be honest with the candidates throughout the process. If they do not make the cut for an RFP, finalist presentation, or winner, tell them straight out.

- Do not take sales calls, during the process, under the guise of additional questions. Simply set aside one day, within the first week after sending out the RFP to conduct 20-minute phone calls with each of the service-provider candidates. In the cover letter, provide a contact name to schedule the phone call, and indicate times will be filled on a first-come/first-served basis.

- Spend an hour or two with an established, unbiased consultant (not an investment advisor/broker) to discuss the state of defined-contribution service providers. They will tell you the inside story of how every provider gets paid and their strengths/weaknesses. They may also provide you a list of the best record-keeping-service-provider candidates, based on your criteria.

- The two most important components of success in a DC plan are communications and investments.

- Watch out for hidden fees or high investment expenses. Focusing solely on out-of-pocket fees may look great for your firm, but be at the expense of the participant, which can lead to future litigation. You have the option to charge administration fees against the trust; hence focus on the total fees. Search consultants are probably best used for clarifying the fees and the service contract.

- If you are going to ask for a completed SAS70, be sure to specify Level II. Many SAS70s are partially self-audited, and I have only run into one or two SAS70 auditors that have actually spent any time as a record-keeping administrator.

Questions to Omit in an RFP

Here are my top five Worthless Questions to ask in an RFP, as you will rarely get a meaningful answer:

1. How many plans were lost in the last year? (*To this day, I have only seen one firm actually put a number in there; and they made my finalists round for being honest. The usual answer from the service providers is we have lost business, but a majority was due to acquisitions, mergers, or plan terminations. Now that tells us a lot.*)

2. If you make the finals, will you agree to pay all expenses for on-site visits for our entire party (including the consultant)? (*Believe it or not, I have seen this request on plans with assets as low as $2 million dollars. Usually the question is asked with no details provided as to the numbers in the party or where they are from. All this does is drive up the costs for all providers.*)

3. Specifically, who will be on the service team? Please provide their resumes. (*It is very difficult to assign a team before being awarded the business. In most cases, the response will simply name the employees with the best resumes and pre-*

sentations skills. I am an advocate of asking about the organizational structure, the compensation/incentive plan, and training programs. It is also crucial to personally meet the team in the final due-diligence phase.)

4. Can you provide a complete fund list (including thousands of gradations of risk and return information), in a certain format? *(Morningstar is available for mutual funds, but if you are asking for information about separately managed funds, use the standard industry information or the fund's own published information.)*

5. Can you send 16 bound copies of your proposal (all over the country)? *(Again, this only drives up the costs, as printing color copies and binding professionally is expensive, up to $500 a packet. Plus, very few people read the actual RFPs, especially when the consultant provides a nice easy-to-read report.)*

Referrals

As we acknowledged earlier, your firm already has trusted advisors such as your auditor, accountant, payroll provider, and HR personnel, many of who may sell their own solution or could recommend one through other partnerships. Ask them to refer you to a plan sponsor who is using your prospective record-keeping service provider.

Be cautious when using the Internet to screen prospective service providers. Few of these websites have true rating systems or actually perform their own research. Remember that some of these websites provide a rating system that is derived wholly from information provided by the service providers, themselves.

It is tough to rate service providers without making on-site visits. However, your trusted advisors, who are not pushing their partners, can certainly tell about client satisfaction (or dissatisfaction) from other plan sponsors.

A Final Word

Don't just go with the first person you meet, or the least expensive route, since hiring the wrong record-keeping service provider can result in costly errors in compliance that may include fines and/or reparations, and loss of confidence with your participants. Perform your due diligence. The key to the due-diligence process (with, or without, a consultant or an advisor) is talking directly with those who perform the work. Get to know the leader of the group and one or two players who may be assigned to your plan. You will be surprised how much you can learn about their day-to-day travails and their approach to customer service.

CHAPTER V

How Does Your Plan Rate?

How Does Your plan rate? Should you be looking for a new service provider or consultant?

When I talk to plan sponsors, most of them have received at least some complaints about their employee benefits — whether they have a defined-contribution, health-benefit or defined-benefit plan. This is to be expected, and the plan's current service provider can resolve most problems. Yet plan sponsors are bombarded with sales calls or e-mails from other service providers offering to fix the problems that exist. I advise more than half of these companies not to get a new service provider.

You should consider moving your plan if two or more of the next five areas are answered 'no' or 'don't know':

1. **The investment menu** — Is someone responsible for monitoring the investment menu to ensure that participants are offered a broad investment spectrum with funds that meet your risk/return criteria? (*If you do not have an investment policy, this answer is 'No'. If somebody is taking great care of that investment menu and meeting with you quarterly or annually, there's no reason for you to look elsewhere.*)

2. **Communications** — Are your participants receiving a consistent and highly rated communication campaign? How often do they come on-site for group meetings or one-on-one contacts? How much information can they get on the Internet? What do they receive in the mail? Do participants have access to on-demand retirement modeling and asset allocation software? Can they tell within 15 minutes if they have enough to retire on, based on what they have in their account and their current contribution rate? (*If that answer is 'No', they're not getting a good communication campaign.*)

3. **Fees** — Have all of your service providers adequately disclosed their fees and complete revenues? If yes, are the fees commensurate with the level of service you are receiving?

4. **Participant satisfaction** — Are your participants generally happy with their service related to the plan (not the company match or profit sharing)? (*This involves surveying the participants, but you don't want the loud minority dictating your decision. I have seen plans with hundreds of participants switch providers because of one or two problem employees. In one case, two disgruntled participants demanded to have a certain fund family, and caused such disruption that the company changed the plan. All for the wrong reasons. They had great technology, great communications, solid compliance — but the company just didn't want to deal with those two people. And it cost the other participants. The plan spent more money in their own internal soft dollars and some out-of-pocket converting that plan.*)

   If you are going to formally survey your participants, make sure the following questions are asked, as they are an excellent indicator of the areas on which you need to focus:

   - Do you know what your realistic retirement goals are? If not, is it because the service provider hasn't worked with you to determine your goals? (If so, we simply need to change the communication campaign.)
   - Are you getting too much or too little communication related to the plan? (This can be asked in a number of ways, but it is important to find out if you are overwhelming them or not providing enough.)
   - Is the system easy to use?

5. **Compliance** — How did you rate the provider? Is the client service team responsive? Do they know their stuff on compliance? Are the plan sponsor reports and the compliance reports accurate and timely? Is the system easy to use? Is it easy to send or download contributions and payroll information? (*Turnover is prevalent in record-keeping service providers, therefore, it is essential there is consistency somewhere on your service team.*)

Ironically, I have interviewed plan sponsors after a conversion, only to find out that they moved their plan when the first four questions were answered positively; but, the fifth question was answered negatively, due to timing of compliance tests and forms. That's really not a reason to move. It's possible that the participants are happy with everything; they know what their retirement goals are; they love the technology and Internet; and they love the 1-800 number. They're getting great communication and the investment menu is fantastic—the employer is just having a problem getting the compliance reports. In that case, the solution is simple: Hire somebody else to do the compliance reports.

Avoid Biased Advice

Various publications—national newspapers, financial journals, industry websites—often come up with easy questionnaires, using a point system to rate responses to questions such as: "How good is your service provider?" Invariably, these questionnaires are skewed to make plan sponsors want to move. In fact, I recently read an article in USA Today that implied that if your plan doesn't have a money-market fund, you might have issues. This is consistent with what other financial journals are implying. But these authors don't know what they're talking about; they don't know the record-keeping industry.

Based on the conservative fund options, plan sponsors are far better off using a stable-value fund than a money-market fund. Stable-value funds are historically 150 basis points higher than money-market funds. Money-market funds are in plans for two reasons: 1) a broker has to be paid; and 2) money managers can say, "I'm not in the market—I'm in money-market funds." Stable-value funds are only available for retirement plans. The contracts and funds are geared for the long term, not day-to-day arbitrage or interest-rate games.

Unfortunately, our popular press isn't as informed as it should be. When rating your plan, answer the questions on the previous page. If in doubt, start talking to qualified experts. They won't charge you for a phone call, as they probably want you for a client. Just don't turn into a 'consultant basher'—that is, one who uses consultants and advisors under the pretense that you might hire them.

CHAPTER VI

Effective Plan Design

The Boring Compliance Stuff—It Is Important!

There are hundreds of books on plan design, many of which are fantastic if you are trying to solve a sweeping issue. The purpose of this section is to give the reader an overview of the plan-design process and high-level look at the types of retirement plans that are out there. Even though Compliance/Plan Design is not exciting to read about (yes, it's boring), if not addressed and done correctly, it can be costly via higher administration fees, or can even threaten the plan's qualification status.

In defined-contribution plans, excellent plan design results in:
- An easy-to-administer plan
- The actual honest goals of the owners (small and private plans) and senior managers (public and large plans) being achieved
- A plan easy to communicate to the employees
- Compliance tests that are easy to perform
- Accurate and timely completion of required documentation, such as the Form 5500

A well-designed plan will be running at its most efficient level, and most likely achieving high satisfaction rates from employees and employers alike.

Effective plan design is not an accident. It is a result of careful planning, expert advice and creative thinking. Proper plan design is an essential part of the success of any qualified retirement program. There are many different types of retirement plans; and, the appropriate document format and plan type depends on many variables including the employer's goals, corporate culture, investment philosophies, investment style and employee demographics.

Plan Sponsor Expectations

Each employer enters into the decision to sponsor a qualified retirement plan based on certain expectations. A few of these expectations include:

- Providing a key part of the compensation package through profit sharing or company matching
- Keeping up with the competition, a throw-in benefit
- Retaining good employees through a vesting schedule or eligibility period

If the expectations are not met, the plan has not done its job. Generally, the 'throw-in' plan is a disaster because the owner, or senior managers, do not really believe in it or promote it properly. From the start, the employer, the employer's service providers, and all other consultants involved in the plan's design and implementation need to be on the same page with respect to the feasibility of a plan, the anticipated costs of operating the plan and the plan's specific objectives. A good consultant or advisor will get right to the point on the reasons for a plan, which is often to maximize the owner's or senior managers' deferred compensation.

Plan-Design Considerations

How do you design the right plan or know if you have the right plan in place? First, be leery of a salesperson who presents a product the first time you meet, OR without completing any due diligence on your organization, in relation to your objectives, company culture, demographics, etc. Many sales people will not complete any plan- design analysis and simply try to sell you a standard 401(k) profit-sharing plan because it is easy. This could lead to poor employee participation, limited owner/highly compensated employee contribution limits, or, worse yet, high contribution requirements by the owner. A provider should never be recommended without first understanding the design of your plan. As a result, the plan will satisfy your objectives and the selected provider will be able to prepare an accurate bid in order to avoid surprises down the road, in terms of cost.

Plan-design software has made tremendous strides in the marketplace. Most importantly, it is very easy to use, even for a novice. In addition, some software providers will charge based on usage (even one time) rather than requiring a large one-time expense and annual fees thereafter. There is no need to hire an attorney or consultant to run expensive projections, when this software is available at a very low price. The attorneys and consultants should be there for assisting you in walking through the process, making the best decision, AND implementing the plan.

Having said that, when plans are designed to maximize an owner's or senior managers' deferred compensation, the plans can become trickier to administer. In fact, very few plan participants in a profit-sharing plan know that their contribution percentage/benefit may actually be lower than that of the owner or senior managers. The best plan-design consultants and record-keeping administrators do an excellent job of not letting participants know this (if they do, they generally get fired). Please remember, good plan design should take into consideration the specific tasks involved in operating the plan on a day-to-day basis. It's unfortunate that they rarely do.

In some cases, the administrative burdens or costs associated with a particular plan design negate the overall value of a provision. However, as indicated in the section of this chapter on RFPs, the plan design is often completed first, so the plan design may be great for a few, but it may drive up costs. This is why it is essential to have a consultant or advisor that understands not only plan design, but also the record-keeping administration process. In order to avoid potential trouble spots, the plan should be looked at from a legal, a strategic and a practical perspective. Each angle will reveal different observations, which must be examined in the aggregate. There is no point in a cost-saving design or allocation if the savings will be eroded by added expense and opportunity for error.

Finally, my pet peeve in the industry is that plan-design consultants and attorneys often complain about the fees and poor service of record keepers (mainly timeliness of difficult company matches or profit-sharing calculations). Keep in mind that record keepers cannot keep costs low when they have to perform work that is not routine. In my opinion, plan sponsors should start charging the plan-design consultants, or attorneys, for record-keeping administration that is not simple to process, when it is not clearly articulated in the sales contract. (This will never happen.)

Step-by-Step Plan Development

Following is a general description of the tasks involved in establishing and operating a qualified retirement plan. Within these general categories are a host of individual responsibilities. The extent that any of these tasks are to be outsourced to third parties should be put in writing with the understanding that the plan sponsor remains ultimately responsible for the overall operation of the plan.

STEP 1: Plan Feasibility

It should be stated that certain employers do not want, or need, a qualified retirement plan. Even for those who do, the following questions should be explored before going forward, to help determine if a qualified retirement plan is feasible, and if so, what would be the most appropriate overall design:

What is the objective of the plan?

Qualified plans are not one-size-fits-all; a plan should be custom fit to the specific needs of the plan sponsor and participants. For example, is the plan intended as a true employee-benefit plan, or a tax shelter, or primarily as part of an executive compensation package? Oftentimes, the decision-makers have different objectives.

Who will participate?

While the decision is invariably going to be made by a few key decision makers, it is essential to solicit input from the employees to determine their interest in participating. This is especially important if the proposed plan is a 401(k) plan, where the success of the program hinges on adequate participation, particularly on the part of the lower-compensated employees. There will be some employees who cannot afford to participate in a qualified retirement plan, and others who simply are more interested in their weekly take-home pay, than in investing or tax savings.

To encourage participation, the plan design can incorporate certain features that are considered important to the non-highly compensated, such as loans, in-service withdrawals, compelling matching contributions on lower deferral percentages (i.e. 100 percent of the first 3 percent, as opposed to 50 percent of the first 6 percent.) Also, as a result of recent tax-law changes, certain participants will be entitled to a tax credit along with the tax-deferred treatment of plan contributions.

In addition to employee interest, other considerations to factor into the plan design include workforce demographics such as age, years of service and compensation.

Does the employer understand and accept the obligations of a plan sponsor?

Sponsoring a qualified plan requires a substantial commitment on the part of the employer. The employer can wear many different hats, but none negate overall fiduciary responsibility to the plan. Some of these "hats" are:

- Plan Sponsor
- Plan Administrator
- Plan Trustee
- Fiduciary
- Plan Participant

While it is not essential for the plan sponsor to become an expert in legal and tax matters, the plan sponsor should be well aware of the basic legal parameters under which a qualified plan must operate, and the consequences for falling outside of those guidelines. Qualified retirement plans operate under the specific guidance of two federal agencies: the Internal Revenue Code and ERISA. In addition, SEC rules and state and local laws can impact plan design and operation. The rules with respect to qualified retirement plans are quite complex and change frequently.

What is the plan budget?

It is crucial that an employer understand the true costs, both fixed and contingent, of establishing and operating a qualified retirement plan. In addition to the obvious costs of employer contributions, there is the annual cost of administration and the time and expense of internal costs involved in administering the plan. The expenses must be reasonable. Care should be taken to assure that services are not being paid for twice. This is a common result of unbundled services that are not properly coordinated. Many of the costs associated with operation of the plan ("trust expenses") can be paid out of the assets of the plan, while some expenses defined by ERISA will remain as "settlor expenses," and as such, are required to be paid outside the plan.

It should also be determined what fees will be payable by the plan participant. The IRS has noted that certain fees cannot be directly assessed to the plan participant. For example, most loan-origination fees are payable by the person taking the loan. But, a participant who is the subject of a qualified domestic-relations order cannot be charged the costs incurred by the plan to process that order.

STEP 2: Plan Construction

Assuming that plan feasibility research proves positive, the next step is to actually design the program. A written plan document is required for any qualified retirement program and should reflect the information gathered in the feasibility study: the plan sponsor's budget, employee demographics, employer and employee expectations, administrative requirements and limitations, and legal requirements.

Specific design elements include:

- Employer
- Employees
- Eligibility
- Automatic enrollment
- Compensation
- Plan year
- Catch-up provisions
- Service crediting
- Contributions
- Requirements for sharing in allocation-nondiscrimination testing
- Vesting
- Safe harbors
- Valuations
- Normal early retirement
- In-service distributions
- Loans
- QJSA QPSA
- 404(c)

Plan Document

Comparison of Document Alternatives

Type of Document	ADVANTAGE	DISADVANTAGE
Custom-Designed Plan	• Drafted to meet specific need of plan sponsor • Addresses operational issues in a specific manner	• Very expensive (initial and ongoing) • Plan has not had preliminary review of the IRS • Must be submitted for a determination letter to assure that the document meets legal requirements • A lot of record keepers will not accept custom-designed plans. Those that do will charge a premium for record-keeping administration unless it fits its standard model
Volume-Submitter Plan	• Lower cost than custom plan • Ability to custom draft with respect to certain issues • Preliminarily reviewed by the IRS • Required updates are often no or low fee	• May not be specific to plan sponsor's special circumstances • May require attorney to review for legal and contractual sufficiency
Prototype Plan	• Easy to prepare • Pre-approved by IRS in most cases • Low cost (often "free") • Two base plan formats to choose from, plus customized adoption agreement	• Very general • Often filled out without attention to detail or clear understanding of the impact of selecting a certain option • It is part of a bundled package, and to keep costs low, the burden of accuracy is on the plan sponsor

Types of Plans

Don't let a salesperson convince you to create a certain type of plan without a plan-design analysis, as their motives are compensation, not creation of the best plan. This is especially true in non-qualified plans that may be backed with insurance. As a side note, plan sponsors often get calls from advisors urging them to set up non-qualified plans, for all of the wrong reasons. Why? To sell insurance. I learned, early on, that the key to success in plan design is to build based on your firm's need, not on what a salesperson tells you. Also, non-qualified plans can be an important component in the overall compensation package for senior managers. Therefore, the most important question to ask when determining if you should implement a non-qualified plan is whether to fund it, or not to fund it (the liability can reside on the corporate books).

There are very few brokers or insurance salespersons who are going to tell you the unfunded approach is best, simply because they cannot get compensated. Also, don't let attorneys play with your plan design and incorporate the latest fad, or create a plan that requires a lot of administrative work, or enhancements to the document, as was popular in the mid-1990s.

As defined earlier, there are two main types of qualified retirement plans that meet the requirements as set forth by the Internal Revenue Code:

- Defined-benefit plans
- Defined-contribution plans

In addition, there are *hybrid* plans that display the characteristics of both types of plans:

- Cash balance
- Target benefit
- Cross-tested defined-contribution

DEFINED-BENEFIT PLANS

The defining characteristic of these plans is that they offer a definitely determinable benefit. The benefit formula is generally stated as a percentage of final average compensation. Some defined-benefit plans offer a specific dollar benefit based on a certain *unit* of service; for example, $100 a month, per year of service. Unit benefit plans are most appropriate in situations where most of the employees are making comparable pay and the goal is to reward longevity.

Defined-benefit plans are most appropriate when the goal is to maximize benefits for older workers. Because the retirement benefit is expressed as a percentage of pay, any contribution made to a defined-benefit plan will weigh more heavily toward older workers.

A defined-benefit plan requires that a pension actuary prepare an annual valuation of the plan's assets, which is among the reasons that this plan is more expensive to operate.

DEFINED-CONTRIBUTION PLANS

Defined-contribution plans are individual account plans. An account is created for each participant, in which contributions are allocated. Unlike defined-benefit plans, in a defined-contribution plan, the plan participant, not the plan sponsor, bears the investment risk.

There are two primary types of defined-contribution plans:

- Profit-Sharing Plans
- Money-Purchase Plans

Profit-Sharing Plans

The defining characteristic of profit-sharing plans is they are designed, for the most part, to provide for a discretionary contribution with a specified allocation. Although the contributions are not required each plan year, the contributions must be substantial and reoccurring. Failure to make substantial and reoccurring contributions will result in the plan not being considered permanent. Following are the types of profit-sharing plans:

- Non-Integrated Profit-Sharing Plan
- Integrated Profit-Sharing Plan
- Age-Weighted Profit-Sharing Plan
- New Comparability Profit-Sharing Plan

There are certain design features that can be added to a profit-sharing plan. 401(k) plans, stock-bonus plans and ESOP programs are types of profit-sharing plans.

401(k) plans are the most popular type of profit-sharing plan. In a 401(k) plan, a participant shares in the funding of the plan by entering into a salary-reduction agreement. A salary-reduction agreement is a written agreement to forego compensation, in lieu of a contribution to the plan. Oftentimes as an incentive to defer, the employer will match the employee deferrals, generally on a stated percentage of the deferral amount (i.e. 50 percent of the first 6 percent of compensation that was deferred).

401(k) plans cannot discriminate in favor of highly compensated employees. A 401(k) is required to pass the Actual Deferral Percentage (ADP) test with respect to employee deferrals and the Actual Contribution Percentage (ACP) test with respect to any employer matching contributions. To avoid these requirements, a 401(k) plan can adopt safe-harbor provisions, which means the employer must provide one of the following minimum contributions:

1. A non-elective employer contribution of 3 percent of compensation for all eligible employees
2. An employer matching contribution of at least 4 percent of an employee's compensation. The basic required match is dollar-for-dollar on the employee deferrals up to 3 percent of pay, and 50¢ per dollar on the next 2 percent of pay. Thus, an employee must defer 5 percent of pay to get this minimum safe harbor 4 percent employer matching contribution.

Please note: *The above minimum contributions are 100 percent vested, immediately.*

In addition, the top-heavy rules will not apply at all to safe harbor 401(k) plans that are salary-deferral-only plans, as long as they meet the above non-elective or matching- contribution formula. However, an employer who is making profit-sharing contributions to a safe harbor 401(k) plan remains subject to the top-heavy rules. If the plan has employer profit-sharing contributions, and is top heavy, and the employer is using the above matching formula, the employer would not have to put in additional money for those 401(k) participants receiving the matching contribution. The employer would still be required to put in 3 percent of compensation for only those non-highly compensated eligible participants who are not contributing to the plan.

Some profit-sharing plans have stock-bonus plans. (*See* Stock-Ownership Plans)

An Employee Stock-Ownership Plan (ESOP) is an employee-benefit plan that makes the employees of a company owners of stock in that company. ESOPs can be either profit- sharing or money-purchase pension plans. Under a profit-sharing ESOP plan, the company agrees to make annual contributions, which may be discretionary (unlike money-purchase ESOPs). Those contributions are invested on behalf of the plan participants in primarily employer stock. Generally, employer contributions may vary from 0 to 25 percent of the total annual eligible payroll and are usually determined after the close of each plan year.

A stock-bonus plan is when a company provides employees its own shares as compensation and/or benefits. In a 401(k) plan, a company may make matching or profit-sharing contributions in the form of stock. The obvious advantage for companies utilizing the stock-bonus plan is they can contribute stock, rather than cash.

The profit-sharing ESOP must satisfy annual nondiscrimination testing guidelines, provide for minimum benefits in any year that the plan is determined to be top heavy and not exceed 25 percent, or $40,000, allocation to a single participant in any one year.

Some features that make ESOPs unique are:
- Only an ESOP is required by law to invest primarily in the securities of the sponsoring employer
- An ESOP is unique among qualified employee-benefit plans in its ability to borrow money. As a result, "leveraged ESOPs" may be used as a technique of corporate finance.

The two most common uses of ESOPs are to buy the stock of a retiring owner in a closely held company, and as an extra employee benefit or incentive plan.

Money-Purchase Plans

A money-purchase plan is a tax-favored plan for all businesses. Unlike other defined-contribution plans, the money-purchase plan has a required employer contribution. This required contribution is an amount stated in the plan document (same percent contribution required each year).

The company makes 100 percent of the contribution; however, a vesting schedule may be implemented. The maximum contribution that an employer can deduct is 25 percent of an employee's pay.

As a result of certain changes in the law due to the Economic Growth and Tax Relief Reconciliation Act (EGTRRA) of 2001, many companies that have both a profit-sharing plan and a money-purchase plan are combining the plans into one 401(k) profit-sharing plan. Why? In the past, companies implemented a profit sharing and money-purchase plan to maximize contributions. In order to get to the 25 percent maximum contribution level, companies could contribute up to 15 percent of an employee's compensation via a profit-sharing plan and make up the 10 percent contribution difference via the money purchase plan. EGTRRA revised the contribution limits to allow companies with profit-sharing plans to contribute up to 25 percent of an employee's compensation. In addition, companies are adopting the 401(k) provision, which allows employees to contribute up to 100 percent of their compensation, or $12,000 (2003), whichever is less. Most importantly, the salary deferrals do not count against the 25 percent maximum contribution limit (up to $40,000). **Bottom Line**: *The cost of having two plans, i.e. the money-purchase plan, is not needed.*

OTHER TYPES OF DEFINED-CONTRIBUTION PLANS

Simplified Employee Pensions Plans (SEP Plans)

A SEP is a tax-favored plan tailored specifically for small businesses and sole proprietors. It can be used by both for-profit and tax-exempt organizations.

A SEP creates an IRA account for each participant. Participants control their own investments, reducing the businesses' fiduciary responsibility; however, the company makes 100 percent of the contribution and vesting is immediate, so it may be less attractive for some employers. SEPs require minimal paperwork, with no annual IRS Form 5500 or Department of Labor filings. Any employee who has worked three out of the previous five years, and is age 21 or older, is eligible for the plan; an employer can exclude an employee whose annual pay is less than $450.

Company contributions of up to 25 percent of an employee's pay are deductible from pretax profits. Contributions are based on an equal percentage of each employee's salary.

Please note: *The Salary Reduction option (SAR-SEP) was eliminated as of 12/31/96. SAR-SEPs established before 12/31/96 can be grandfathered in.*

Savings Incentive Match Plan for Employees (SIMPLE)

A SIMPLE is a tax-favored plan tailored specifically for small businesses with no more than 100 employees and sole proprietors. It can be used by both for-profit and tax-exempt organizations.

Similar to a SEP, a SIMPLE creates an IRA account for each participant. Unlike SEPs, SIMPLE plans allow for employees to defer money into the plan, and participants control the investment selection. However, the company is required to make one of the following contributions:

1. Employers can match each participant's compensation, dollar for dollar, up to 3 percent of their annual pay. (With this option, the overall match can be reduced to as little as 1 percent of participants' annual pay in two out of five years.)
2. Employers can make a non-elective contribution of 2 percent of eligible employees' gross annual pay. The employee's compensation limit is $200,000.

Similar to SEP plans, the employer contribution is 100 percent vested immediately. Employers are able to decide their contribution option for each year. The matching option allows contributions to be made at the same time as participant deferrals, or as a lump sum payment at the end of the plan year. The non-elective option allows contributions to be made in a lump sum at the end of the plan year. Contributions under both options must be remitted by the employer's tax filing deadline, including extensions.

In relation to contribution limits, in 2003, employees can contribute up to $8,000 on a tax-deferred basis. Those who are age 50 and over can contribute up to an additional $500.

STEP 3: Ongoing Operation and Processing

The two key questions at this stage are: What needs to be done, and who is going to do the work? Once the various tasks have been identified, they should be delegated (in writing) to appropriate parties. The responsible party should acknowledge the specific duties with respect to those assigned tasks.

Key Tasks
- Implementing the specific terms of the document
- Developing written policies and procedures
- Accurate census and data collection
- Availability of correction programs under both the IRS and the DOL
- Compliance with IRS rules and regulations, ERISA claims and reporting and disclosure
- Coordination with other labor laws
- Compliance with General Trust Law
- Determining the need for, or selecting, prudent experts

The overall administrative process, based on the plan-design choices, must be outlined. From this outline, form a "to-do" list. At this point, written policies and procedures are essential. Carefully drafted service agreements are equally important.

STEP 4: *Compliance Testing*

Compliance testing is the process of reviewing the overall operation of the plan with respect to its ongoing qualification (as determined by ERISA). It also includes performance of certain nondiscrimination tests. The key to quality compliance testing is the accuracy of the data. The ease of data collection should be considered during the plan-design process. Periodic self-audit is essential to the ongoing successful operation of a qualified retirement plan.

The basic review process includes the following:

- Review of plan documents
- Review of administrative and operational procedures
- Review of forms and plan-related files

Every record-keeping service provider has the capability to perform all of the required tests; however, due diligence requires a focus on the following:

- What level of employee performs the tests and reviews them? Is there a dedicated group, or does the processing team perform the tests?
- Are the tests performed from the record-keeping system, compliance-only software, or spreadsheets? (*You might be surprised at how many firms use the latter for testing.*)

- Who actually signs off on the test—the record-keeping service provider or the plan sponsor? (*Some firms actually ask the plan sponsor to sign off on the test.*)
- What is their standard turnaround on projected and final tests? Will they guarantee the turnaround time?
- Do they require year-end input in a special format, even though they store the data on the system?
- Who tracks highly compensated employees?
- How many of the Form 5500s are extended?
- Do they perform financial summaries?

Bottom Line: *Interview the personnel who will be performing the tasks.*

Most common compliance mistakes:

- Failing to file the Form 5500
- Failing to properly determine when employees are eligible to participate in a qualified retirement plan
- Incorrect calculation of vesting percentage
- Failing to provide requisite notice and election forms
- Excluding part-time employees from participation
- Failing to properly compute the maximum annual limitations on contributions, or to properly calculate the deductible contribution for the plan year
- Failing to amend the plan for new laws
- Incorrectly performing coverage and nondiscrimination tests, and failing to make timely corrections

Any sized company should hire a specialist to perform the compliance tasks, including plan design, if necessary. This is what has made the TPA model and the large-plan consultants successful. **Bottom Line**: *No one should be afraid of compliance; if they are, they will be taken advantage of, in relation to fees.*

Disclosure can be categorized into three general categories:

1. Required disclosures
2. Disclosures made available upon request
3. Materials available for inspection

STEP 5: Record Retention

Record retention is an often-overlooked function of a plan's overall operation. It is critical that plan sponsors keep complete and accurate records. The IRS and the DOL maintain active field-audit staff who may audit a plan to ensure that deductions are proper and that participants are treated fairly. The records in support of a plan's annual reporting and disclosure generally must be retained for a period of six years after the documents to which they relate are filed with the applicable governmental agencies. Dates and signatures must be clearly visible.

In conclusion, plan design is where it all starts. If we were to informally poll plan sponsors (especially in the small-plan market), a majority would say that the person who sold them the plan was the one that designed it for them.

Some plan sponsors who have been burned take the opposite approach. I call them 'consultant or advisor bashers' (as referred to previously). They ask record keepers to do all of the plan preparation, under the pretense that they might be hired, later, to service the plan; but they never are. Therefore, if you are a record-keeping service provider, there is an art to knowing where to stop.

Bottom Line: *Plan sponsors must follow this approach, and record-keeping service providers must understand all of the components as well.*

CHAPTER VII

The Investment Menu

Investment Management — Don't Take It Lightly

Investment management is clearly the most important component of selecting a defined-contribution provider, with participant communications a close second. Achieving a successful retirement income level by utilizing a 401(k) plan starts early, with a strong communication campaign and quality investment fund offerings. Many plan participants fall into the category of the "uninformed investor," or may be too young to appreciate planning for retirement. With this in mind, a plan sponsor is faced with a difficult question: "What funds should we offer and how many?" Too many fund choices may confuse the participant; too few may not allow for a successful retirement strategy. Furthermore, the plan sponsor needs to be thinking of retirement distribution options, as opposed to just providing a distribution form and hoping they leave the plan.

Six Types of Investment Options

As a review, there are typically six types of investment options available for plan sponsors:

- Mutual Funds
- Collective Investment Funds (CIFs)
- Separately Managed Funds
- Asset-Allocation Funds or Lifestyle Funds
- Individually Directed Accounts (IDAs)
- Company Stock

At distribution time, a plan sponsor should offer the following:

- **Rollover Access** — Easy access to a rollover account (hopefully with the same funds available)

- **Fixed Annuity** — The ability to purchase an annuity that guarantees a monthly income in the retirement years

Mutual Funds

Mutual Funds are the most prevalent of the options selected by defined-contribution sponsors. The Securities and Exchange Commission (SEC) directly regulates these funds. Investment management fees are taken out at the daily net asset value (NAV) at the same rate for every dollar invested. In the late 1980s, mutual funds were the cutting edge trend, as participants could track their investments in the newspaper. Unfortunately for the participant, the trend in the mutual-fund industry is to have multiple classes for each fund, with the class used for the plan dependent on sales commissions or the service-provider selected. Class A is generally the best, as front-end sale charges are usually waived, and the investment/expense ratio is typically the lowest. Multiple share classes make tracking difficult. With tracking issues and high investment fees in a lot of mutual funds, separately managed funds are becoming popular again (for all of the right reasons, i.e., lower investment/expense ratios). Watch out for Class B or C shares, as these typically have higher investment fees and/or back-end loads (back). A quick review:

- **Class A** — These shares are sold with an up-front sales charge, which declines as the amount invested increases. In addition, sales charges are waived for plans with $1,000,000 or more in assets. In addition, some platforms waive front-end sale charges, regardless of plan size. Generally, A-shares carry a lower annual expense ratio than other share classes.

- **Class B** — Instead of an up-front sales charge, B-shares have a contingent deferred sales charge (CDSC). This charge is paid only if shares are redeemed within the first X years (6 years is the most common) of purchase. B-shares carry a higher expense ratio, which is generally contributed to a higher 12b-1 fee that is paid to the investment advisors. In addition, B-shares usually convert to Class A-shares after X years (8 years is the most common), or when the plan reaches a certain dollar amount.

- **Class C** — Often called level-load shares, as they do not have an up-front sales charge; however, they do have a 1 percent contingent deferred sales charge (CDSC) on shares redeemed within 12 months of purchase. Similar to B-shares, C-shares carry a higher expense ratio, which is generally contributed to a higher 12b-1 fee that is paid to the investment advisors.

Some fund families will offer a fourth class of funds and some funds will use different names or letters for this fourth class, such as:

- **Class D, F** — Generally, this share class has neither an up-front nor a contingent deferred sales charge, however they will incur a higher expense ratio than A shares. Most traditional broker-dealers now offer fee-based programs that permit investors to purchase mutual funds for an annual asset-based fee, rather than paying commissions or sales charges. This type of share class provides this opportunity. However, as mentioned, not all funds offer this class.

- **Class Y, I** — I shares, or Y-shares, are how institutional shares are designated. Institutional shares are not available to the retail investor unless they are included in a 401(k) plan. Generally, they tend to carry fairly low annual expenses.

- **Class R, K** — R-shares, and K-shares, have neither an up-front nor a contingent deferred sales charge; however, they will incur a higher expense ratio than A-shares and this expense ratio will vary depending on the subclasses. For example, one fund-family has five R-share classes ranging from R-1 to R-5 with varying expense ratios, depending on the plan's asset size. In a nutshell, this mutual fund class is essentially a "create your own" revenue sharing I class

Collective Investment Funds (CIFs)

Collective Investment Funds (CIFs) are typically offered by banks and insurance companies, and are similar to mutual funds, except the Office of the Comptroller of the Currency (OCC) regulates them, instead of the SEC. CIFs have been the vehicle of choice since the inception of the funds in the late 1980's because they offer flexible fee arrangements (lower asset-based fees for clients) and are less expensive to operate.

The key benefit of CIFs is that the fees are variable and typically graduated. CIFs can charge a different fee for each client or charge on an asset-based graded basis. The beauty of this graduated fee schedule is that asset power can lower the overall investment expense charged to the plan. A majority of Stable-Value Funds (previously referred to as GIC Funds) in today's plans are CIFs. With today's technology, participants can visit the record-keeping website or call a 1-800 number to review their account balance, which may bring CIFs back into play.

Separately Managed Funds

Separately Managed Accounts have investment managers who will manage a fund for a plan exclusively, or invest in a pool with other plans (similar to CIFs). The advantage is lower investment advisory fees and a manager who places minimum investments (by plan), thus eliminating the retail issues involved with investing (turnover and chasing rankings). For plans that are direct, no assets are shared with other institutions or retail clients. Separately managed accounts also allow for performance-based investment fees. With today's technology, the fees can be taken out of the record-keeping value, daily, at the manager or record-keeping level. The majority of separate account managers have a minimum of dollars they will manage, ranging from $1 to $20 million, based on the type of fund and/or manager. With today's difficulties in tracking mutual funds, and the advent of the Internet enabling participants to check their accounts and to research investments, separately managed funds will become more popular.

Lifestyle or Asset-Allocation Funds

Lifestyle or Asset-Allocation Funds (Objective Based Funds) are finally catching on as a supplement to the traditional mutual-fund approach. Companies generally offer three asset classes: conservative, moderate, and aggressive. Some managers use a fund of funds (multiple mutual funds within each category); others manage these in a non-mutual fund environment such as CIFs or separately managed accounts. These funds are popular for participants who do not have time to understand the markets, but can fill out a simple questionnaire in order to find out which risk category fits their lifestyle. The good questionnaires ask not only about the participant's risk, but also focus on the participant's net worth and age. *Bottom line: These are great funds for defined-contribution plans, as they can reduce the anxiety risk factor for many participants who are uncomfortable with investing.*

The "fund of funds" asset-allocation approach will have two layers of fees: the underlying mutual-fund expense, plus the investment expense for managing the fund, however the fees are combined and illustrated as one fee.

Individually Directed Accounts (IDAs)

Individually Directed Accounts (IDAs) allow participants to buy and sell any mutual fund or security available in the retail market, or in simple terms, these are brokerage accounts (or known as self-directed accounts (SDAs) and personal choice accounts (PCAs). Plans offering IDAs generally limit these to one brokerage firm, and all transactions by the participant are made directly with the online brokerage firm. In the past, service providers did not have an integrated process to allow for IDAs; therefore, the record keeper and/or the trustee charged annual fees ranging from $50 to $300 a year for the account. These fees do not include commissions on stock transactions, or transaction fees for some mutual funds. Today, IDAs are rapidly becoming an integrated solution for plan sponsors. If implemented correctly, the brokerage account is integrated directly with the directed trustee and/or record-keeping system.

Although IDAs have been around for years, they have never really caught on as a mainstream approach. The reasons are simple: record keepers and/or trustees charge exorbitant fees to allow IDAs in plans, and the year-end Form 5500 and annual audit are difficult to complete, as IDAs are not integrated seamlessly between record keeping and trustee systems. On top of the record-keeping issues, traditionalists proclaim that due to their poor investments, IDAs in plans increase the risk of lawsuits, down the road, from participants.

Company Stock

This menu option offers company stock to participants. Some companies pay all, or a portion, of their company match, or profit sharing, in company stock.

Fiduciary Responsibility

Who is a fiduciary?

First, let's establish, unequivocally, that the company and its corporate trustees WILL always retain fiduciary responsibility. The only code that addresses the fiduciary, related to the investment menu, is ERISA Section 404(c), which was implemented over 10 years ago as a means to move defined-contribution plans out of a one-fund approach, and provide participants more flexibility to transfer funds. A lot of consultants and providers actually believe that this code provides complete protection for the plan sponsor in relation to investment fiduciary lawsuits. In addition, because Section 404(c) is so expansive, ambiguous and expensive, it is virtually impossible to be a 404(c) compliant plan. Read closely, the code indicates it reduces, NOT eliminates, fiduciary responsibility —and today it is out of date. The code does imply that the plan sponsor is not responsible for their participants' investment decisions if they comply with ERISA 404(c). But, because the code is so complex, many consultants and service providers have reverted to the trick of writing on all legal documents a statement that "this plan is a Section 404 (c) intended plan." Of course, that is a polite way of saying that if they miss something, they can always fall back on the fact that they said they intended to.

Here is a list of service entities that say they are not fiduciaries:

- **Directed Trustees** — ("We only clear trades on behalf of the plan.")
- **Record-keeping service providers and TPAs** — ("We are transaction takers.")
- **Attorneys** — ("We just design the plans.")
- **Mutual Funds** — ("Someone else selects the funds for the plan.")
- **Brokers** — ("We don't actually pick the funds.") (Yes, its true.)
- **Plan Participant** — While ultimately responsible for their selections, you can be assured some will blame the plan sponsor if they do not have enough money at retirement (although based on some of the cases I have reviewed, the real cause was the participant not saving enough money).

Who does that leave? The plan sponsor. What should you do as a plan sponsor, knowing you can't eliminate your fiduciary responsibility?

First and foremost, work with an investment advisor, broker or consultant who is willing to tell it like it is. The goal should be to pick the best funds (risk/ return characteristics and past performance) with the lowest investment expense. Most companies have employees of all ages; therefore, you will need to cover the broad investment spectrum, ensuring they have an investment menu that will allow them to build their asset allocation strategy based on their investment objectives.

Now, having said this, here is where the fiduciary liability really lies:

- Any record-keeping service provider that limits their fund menu to funds that pay them (if the funds are inappropriately priced, as compared to the rest of the market)

- Any directed trustee or clearing firm that alters their price to use their proprietary products (money-market funds or Stable-Value Funds)
- Any broker or investment advisor who sells a plan to a plan sponsor and selects funds that benefit themselves (a commission)

All of the above will argue vehemently that they are not fiduciaries. However, they do have culpability for the above actions, and class-action suits are a heck of lot more dangerous than the DOL!

From my point of view, as discussed earlier, it's time for these firms to honestly address their role. If they disclose everything in the sales process, it is hard to Monday-morning-quarterback. Therefore, step one is to hire someone who is clear about their responsibilities and role in helping you with your fund menu. Any firm that is willing to take a co-fiduciary role is a step in the right direction.

Six Easy Steps for Successful Investment Management

Now follow this easy six-step process:

1. Pick the funds; make sure all revenue-sharing dollars are tracked and that all interested parties sign off on their compensation from the funds, including those that do not take compensation and those that take soft dollars, such as marketing fees.
2. Create an investment policy that has easy-to-use (and fair) benchmarks.
3. Hire a service provider who can accommodate your approach.
4. Communicate the decision process to your participants.
5. Monitor the funds quarterly, internally, or through your advisor, consultant, or broker (make them write their thoughts on paper). Communicate with your participants by utilizing your record-keeping service provider and advisors/consultants.
6. Always do the right thing!

Why Exclude a Fund?

Even after you have crossed every "t" and dotted every "i," someone will surely ask:

"Why can't we have this fund in the plan?" To answer the question directly, the fund may not be included for the following reasons:

- A broker or investment advisor may not be able to receive commissions from that fund.
- The record-keeping service provider does not have access to it or does not offer it.

To clarify, investment advisors who charge an investment advisory fee generally work with record-keeping service providers that have access to the entire universe of funds and, in many cases, will take on fiduciary responsibility for selecting and monitoring the funds.

This is why you may want to perform a record-keeping service provider search in conjunction with picking your investment menu.

What Is the Right Number of Funds?

There is no "magic bullet" answer; however, the more funds a plan offers, the more confusing it is for the participant. The average plan today has 12 funds. I have seen plans with 40-50 funds, which are a nightmare to communicate, especially if no one is providing advice at the participant level.

The optimal plan design:

- Ten-15 mutual funds, or separately managed funds, covering the broad investment classes (especially if an advisor or record-keeping service provider is taking fiduciary responsibility for the selection and monitoring)
- One of the 10-15 funds must be a conservative option that does not lose money; therefore, a Stable-Value Fund should be selected (not a money-market fund)
- Three-4 asset-allocation funds, OR the ability for participants to easily create their own asset-allocation funds
- IDAs (with the waiver)

Money Market or Stable-Value Fund?

Choosing the conservative fund in your menu cannot be taken lightly anymore! In the last ten years, this decision has not been an important one, as participants were investing primarily in equity funds. With participants not trusting the equity markets today (and for at least the next five years, as they have long memories), it has now become an important decision. In the past, directed trustees would put their money market or stable value fund solution in, simply because it paid them a lot of money. No one was looking at returns in these funds, so it was not a big deal. Today it is a big deal, and the only two reasons your plan would include a money-market fund are:

- A broker wants to get paid
- The person who designed the plan read somewhere that all plans should have a money-market fund, because professional money managers invest in these funds when they don't like the marketplace.

What is wrong with the last statement? The money managers don't have access to Stable-Value Funds.

The definitions of the funds are as follows:

Money-market funds are the safest type of mutual funds if you are worried about the risk of losing your principal. Money-market funds are like bank savings accounts in that the value of your investment does not fluctuate.

Stable-Value Funds deliver safety and stability by preserving principal and accumulated earnings. They are similar to money-market funds but offer considerably higher returns by investing in GIC's and BIC's. Their returns make them comparable to intermediate bonds, minus the volatility. They are available in defined-contribution plans and, most recently, in Individual Retirement Accounts.

History of Stable-Value Funds

A quick history of stable-value funds is in order. When I first entered the marketplace, stable-value-type investments were returning above 10 percent annually. From an investment advisor perspective, if a return is projected to be 10 percent, with low risk, this is close to a no-brainer. Defined-contribution and defined-benefit plans totaled over $7 trillion in total retirement assets, of which Stable-Value Funds had over $265 billion as of December 2001. In the mid 1980s, stable-value assets garnered over 50 percent of all retirement assets; however, in the late 1980s, these assets started to transfer away from Stable-Value Funds for several reasons:

- Increased participant communications, with emphasis on asset allocation
- ERISA Section Code 404(c) diversification (requires plans to have at least three distinct funds to lower plan-sponsor fiduciary responsibility)
- Issues in the GIC Industry with two major defaulting GIC issuers
- Record-keeping technology advancements allowing participant account balances to be updated daily, while Stable-Value Funds were priced monthly (Stable-Value Funds are collective investment funds that could not be priced daily until the mid- 1990s) and may or may not be mutual funds that are popular in defined-contribution plans
- A long bull market from the late 1980s through 2000

Today, Stable-Value Funds are back in vogue and, per the Stable-Value Investment Association, will garner over 20 percent of all retirement assets by the end of 2003, for the following reasons:

- Due to operational improvements of CIFs, plans with less than $10 million are adding Stable Value Funds. (In fact, five Stable-Value Fund managers are trading on the NSCC platform, which is the equivalent of DTC on Wall Street, and is processed similarly to mutual funds.)
- New contributions to stable value funds from participants are in exces of 50 percent because of marketplace uncertainty.
- Stable-Value Funds are finding ways to provide incentives to advisors and accept IRA rollovers.
- The small-plan marketplace and brokers are demanding access to Stable-Value Funds as a solution to money-market fund low yields (some money-market funds have negative returns after commissions).

Watch out for Stable-Value mutual funds, because most of them have been started in the last few years, with interest rates at an all time low. I don't care how badly a broker wants to get paid, putting monies in a Stable-Value mutual fund instead of a collective investment fund is not thinking of the participant first. The CIFs have higher returns because they have broader portfolios that have been around a long time. If you have to use a mutual fund, review the portfolio risk of the Stable Value Fund, as they are more susceptible to interest-rate movements.

As depicted on the chart to the right, there is no reason a prudent decision maker on the behalf of a defined-contribution plan would select a money-market fund over a Stable-Value Fund.

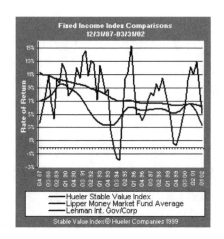

Why Not Have Brokerage Accounts?

To begin with, your record keeper may not offer these; or, if they do, it may be cost-prohibitive. If you have an investment advisor or broker, they typically do not get paid on these monies.

Brokerage accounts are not right for everyone, but certainly offer more freedom to the educated investor. In the last ten years, professional service firms such as physician groups, accountants, engineers, and lawyers have led the way in offering IDAs as part of their plan. In today's defined-contribution environment, it is hard to satisfy every participant, let alone pick 10-12 mutual funds for your plan out of the 9,000 possible mutual funds. In addition to participants wanting more selection, the advertising campaigns of the online brokerage firms are creating a new demand for online brokerage accounts within defined-contribution plans (albeit the technology and market drop in 2001 has cooled plan sponsors and participants on IDAs).

This puts many of the defined-contribution experts in a tough position. On the one hand, it is contrary to everything they have learned from experience: plan for the long-term and stick with your asset-allocation plan. On the other hand, if implemented correctly, IDAs can actually allow more participants to reach their retirement goals. From the plan sponsor perspective, Section 404(c) is becoming outdated and does not offer the total elimination of future litigation related to the investment perspective of the plan. Each year the top defined-contribution surveys continue to tell us that the average number of funds in plans is increasing.

Where does this leave the plan sponsor in relation to IDAs? It is actually very simple. Three to five years down the road, if IDAs are implemented correctly, they will be the standard of defined-contribution plans. Opponents, or traditionalists, will actually become proponents of IDAs, when IDAs can be introduced cost-effectively and in a manner that may actually reduce the risk of future litigation.

With the right service provider, the IDA can be an excellent supplement to your investment menu, as well as rounding out your participant-communication process.

Should Bad Funds Be Replaced?

There are three schools of thought:

1. Don't get rid of a bad fund, because it is best to buy low and sell high; plus, we were told to invest for the long term.
2. Keep the fund, and add another like fund.
3. Replace it.

If you have an investment policy in place, and it has realistic criteria established for monitoring each fund, then you should replace a bad fund. However avoid the "knee jerk" reaction of replacing a fund after one quarter of inferior performance. Be sure to keep the appropriate time horizons and benchmarks in mind when reviewing a fund's performance. With that in mind, avoiding to eliminate a bad fund that does not perform according to the criteria established in the investment policy leaves the plan sponsor wide open for future litigation. This is true even if the fund does turn around after it is replaced, as good investment policies are not too restrictive. Furthermore, if you offer an IDA, then the fund can be purchased there.

What Are the Asset Classes?

The following is an 'Equity Style Box,' which illustrates the different equity asset classes:

Style boxes have been popularized by Morningstar, the ubiquitous mutual-fund rating organization. Morningstar's style box, started in 1992, features nine boxes in a tic-tac-toe grid as depicted on the next page.

THE EQUITY STYLE BOX

Large Cap Value	Large Cap Blend	Large Cap Growth
Mid Cap Value	Mid Cap Blend	Mid Cap Growth
Small Cap Value	Small Cap Blend	Small Cap Growth

There are many resources that allow consultants, financial advisors and plan sponsors access to asset-class information, including the prospectus of any specific mutual fund. When reviewing asset classes, pay close attention to the asset-class history, commonly known as 'style drift.' For example, style drift occurs when a large-cap growth manager drifts from growth stocks and begins to buy another asset class to keep and/or enhance performance as the markets change. Style drift results in increased risk to a participant's asset-allocation strategy, as they can become over-weighted/under-weighted in a specific asset class.

Style drift is crucial during your ongoing monitoring of funds, as you don't want to have 12 distinct funds on Day 1, and then in two years have seven large-cap funds. As mentioned, when building a solid investment menu, focus on selecting funds that cover each (or a majority) of the asset classes. Most importantly, avoid creating an investment menu with three large-cap growth funds (because the performance looks great) and no large-cap value funds. It is impossible to determine which asset class will perform best in any given time period, so allowing your participants the ability to create an asset- allocation strategy with multiple asset classes is the key to their success in reaching their retirement goals. Allowing them to diversify into three large-cap growth funds does nothing for the participant in terms of reducing risk.

For plan sponsors focusing on investment expenses, they can select index or passively managed funds. Index funds track certain indexes such as the S&P 500 for low investment expenses. Passively managed funds buy the entire style (all large-cap funds for example) at very low fee. Both index and passively managed funds are for the plan sponsor that does not believe active managers add value (stock picking and market timing).

Following is a brief review of the terms you may hear:

Growth stocks are defined as funds that buy stocks that have prospects of exceeding the growth of the economy. Growth companies typically sell at high price/earnings (P/E) ratios, reflecting the expectation that their growth will continue and "catch up" with the high valuations.

Value stocks have low book-to-market ratios, which means the stock is trading at a low price compared to its book value. Book value is defined as the company's assets on a balance sheet, less its liabilities, and is often figured on a per-share basis. If a company has a book value of $15 per share, and the stock trades at $12, it may be perceived as a bargain.

Market capitalization indicates the size (the value of a corporation as determined by multiplying the market price of its stock by the shares traded) of the companies in which a mutual fund is investing.

- **Large Cap** invests in stocks of large companies with an average capitalization of approximately $5 billion or greater.
- **Mid Cap** invests in stocks of mid-sized companies with an average capitalization of between $1 billion and $5 billion.
- **Small Cap** invests in stocks of smaller companies with an average capitalization of less than $1 billion.

International Funds are funds that invest primarily in foreign companies. As we transition to a global economy, diversification is best across the globe, not just across the styles mentioned above in U.S. companies alone. As a side note, many of the mutual funds in the above style box will invest in foreign companies, such as Phillips, Nestle, etc.

Emerging Market Funds focus their investments on those economies that are still developing and growing. These are some of the most volatile funds. These are the companies with big pay-offs (or no pay-offs, as when the company folds).

Balanced Mutual Funds — Generally, these funds include two or more asset classes other than cash. In a typical balanced mutual fund, the asset classes are equities and fixed-income securities.

Fixed-Income Funds — The advertised investment objectives of fixed-income funds are safety and income, rather than capital appreciation, but we're skeptical. Income funds invest in corporate bonds or government-insured mortgages; if they own any stocks at all, these are usually preferred shares. The danger is chasing higher yields and not looking at the risks.

Why Early Planning for Distributions and Retirement Is Important

The last thing you want to do is to provide your employees a great investment menu and then tell them "adios" at distribution time. This is also true from the record-keeping service provider's perspective, as they create strategies to retain revenue, especially when the baby-boomers start withdrawing money. Ten years from now, a typical plan will experience net outflow, as opposed to a majority of plans today with net inflow. Instead, make it easy for them to move their monies to a rollover, or to purchase a fixed annuity at retirement. Back in the old days of defined-contribution plans, we used to offer a version of an annuity option that allowed employees to take monthly payments directly from the plan. The reason this is not offered anymore is that record keepers were terrible at administering this option, making overpayments on a regular basis. Making fixed annuities (a better label) available as income replacement to your participants is as simple as processing loans today. Do not be afraid to offer them, as the DOL is making waves that defined-contribution plans should look and act more like defined-benefit plans. Here is an overview.

Income replacement is important to the plan participants who have (or soon will have) reached the end of their peak earning years, and who have a unique set of concerns. They generally have a shorter time for their investments to remain undisturbed and a significantly different risk profile than other investors in the company retirement plan. We use the term "transitioning investors" to describe this group of plan participants. For these plan participants, income replacement is either an immediate need or will be a need in the near future.

While this group of investors may want to continue to seek long-term appreciation on some of their investments, preservation of principal and income replacement have become primary goals for at least a portion of the assets they have accumulated to date. As the average life expectancy for Americans continues to increase, income replacement is a growing concern among the retiring and retired population. An immediate fixed annuity is a product that is well equipped to meet the needs of income replacement, as it is a guarantee that payments will continue for a selected period, which may include the annuitant's lifetime, as well as that of a beneficiary.

Immediate annuities also avoid lump-sum tax impact and probate problems. An immediate fixed annuity, also referred to as a single-premium immediate annuity, is a contract between you and an insurance company. An immediate fixed annuity offers a guaranteed monthly income, for a specific term, regardless of economic conditions. That means the insurance company bears the investment risk associated with a fixed annuity. Immediate fixed annuities are used by people who wish to convert an asset into a stream of income tailored to their needs. The benefits are determined at the time of purchase and are guaranteed for a certain term, such as 10 or 15 years—or for life.

An immediate fixed annuity provides a secure, tax-advantaged way to receive income from assets. Purchasing an immediate annuity requires a one-time premium payment, and income payments usually begin soon after the purchase. Immediate annuities provide unique diversification benefits. When you purchase an immediate annuity with a portion of your retirement assets, you effectively create a secure income foundation. This strategy allows participants to continue investing the remainder of their retirement assets with a longer time in mind, which will help guard against the possibility of outliving their investments.

An immediate annuity is an insurance product that provides a guarantee of income and security that other investments do not. It can provide lifelong income, thus reducing the risk of outliving one's resources. Like a growing number of transitioning investors, you may want to consider the guarantees of an immediate fixed annuity as part of your retirement-planning process.

However, it is imperative that fixed annuities are purchased using institutional pricing, with competition, as opposed to just accepting the first bid. There are two solutions to getting the best price: hire a consultant to perform a search, or have participants use Income Solutions (the only competitive bidding process via the Internet).

Income Solutions

Income Solutions is the only program available that allows individuals, independent of their employer, to convert a portion of their retirement assets to a guaranteed income stream through the purchase of an institutionally priced immediate annuity. Individuals can benefit from the same competitive bidding process and pricing that large institutional buyers have access to; and, they can choose not only the annuity terms that best meet their needs, but can select the annuity provider as well. Annuity quotes requested through Income Solutions are each competitively bid, and priced as though the individual were a large institutional buyer.

The illustration to the right, shows the approximate benefits an individual can expect to receive when institutional pricing and competitive bidding are combined. If you are a 60-year-old male, purchasing a $100,000 Life Income Annuity, with a 10-year-period certain, on average you would receive $690 a month when purchasing an annuity on the Income Solutions platform or through a consultant, versus $630 a month buying a traditional retail annuity. This is over an 8.5 percent difference, or a $60 increase in your monthly payment. When taking into consideration the effect of compounding interest, the approximate difference over a 10-year period is $8,000; over 20 years it is approximately $23,000, and over 30 years, the difference grows to over $42,000.

The Income Solutions platform removes all added retail costs and the confusing hype associated with buying annuities. All quotes are provided on a net basis. This means that when an individual receives a quote, there are no added costs; the monthly income quote reflects all costs associated with a provider's participation in the program. The Income Solutions program is dedicated solely to providing individuals with immediate annuity quotes and related information.

Why offer company stock when the national press says it is a bad option?

Why do we have to regulate common sense when it comes to offering company stock in a defined-contribution plan?

- **One in five 401(k) participants have more than 20 percent of their plan in company stock.**
- **94.7 of Proctor and Gamble DC participants are in company stock.**

Enron is not the first company to have issues with company stock in their defined-contribution plan, nor will it be the last. Each time we have an event similar to Enron, our popular press cries for reform and our government tries to oblige. The last go-around in the early 1990s was to add diversification clauses to company matches, and ESOPs, once a participant had attained a certain age. Recently, our current government has suggested diversification after a period of three years (for company matches). This may be good stuff for making people feel good; however, it begs the question of why don't companies, and those who advise them, do what is right in the first place?

The common-sense approach begins with those who serve the plan sponsor, including attorneys, accountants, banks, record keepers, and investment advisors. Many of these play the role of influencer and, in some cases, are the key influencers. Since all of these firms are in the customer-service business, in order to become more profitable it is essential that the client is happy, which can be a conflict of interest. This allows these firms to potentially sell more services to the client, as well as to gain more clients through good word of mouth. Ultimately, the influencers will benefit by persuading their clients to do what is right for the plan participants.

In my experience as a consultant designing plans, it is a very rare for a small company owner, or a large company, to act in an altruistic manner. Most small-business owners, when creating defined-contribution plans, design plans that favor themselves. Large corporations create non-qualified plans and incorporate stock options to attract and maintain senior managers, again placing themselves first. The simple truth is that most companies no longer offer employee benefits as perks; they are more of a requirement to attract and retain employees. The bottom line is literally the bottom line, as employee benefits are part of the overall compensation package. Hence, plan design becomes even more critical to maximize the value of a company's human-resource dollar.

With plan design playing a greater role, company stock adds an increased perceived benefit to employees (the dream of hitting it big, or as I call it, the lottery-ticket effect). In fact, I am a believer in ESOPs, company-match-in-stock, and stock option or bonus plans. These plans are only as strong as they are honest. Company stock is a risk, and it should be communicated as such. But, for every negative story related to company stock, I can tell you a good one. As influencers with our clients in the retirement industry, let's always remember the plan participant, as they are the heart and soul of the company.

110

The Investment Menu

Here are a few items to consider as influencers:

- A company match is not a guaranteed right in a plan; some participant communication specialists call this free money when it is offered as a match. Participants invest their 401(k) deferrals in the funds of their choice, and the company match, invested in company stock, is not a bad thing.
- If all of the employees believe in the company (including senior management), companies should not have any issue allowing participants to transfer their vested portion. At that point, it is their money. Why put in a three-year rule, when common sense dictates using the vesting schedule, as this will not require record keeping or software providers to perform extensive programming (with the entire cost passed on to the participants).
- ESOP plans should have more favorable diversification rules that allow employees to transfer out of the ESOP to the 401(k) plan after the monies are 100% vested. This may not help the company stock, but it does place the employee first.

Obviously companies do not want massive sales of company stock, especially from employees; though, if the company is strong, there will always be buyers. However, defined-contribution plans are not the greatest issue our industry and government has to face in relation to company stock; it is stock options. The following are suggestions that should be implemented immediately:

- When stocks plummet, companies should not be able to re-price options (or reissue new ones)
- Change accounting standards—Currently, options do not count against profits. In Enron's case, the deductions would have amounted to over $2 billion in the period from 1998-2000, which was slightly less than the reported profits.
- Issue options at the current market price—not below it. Why should executives be rewarded for the stock staying flat? These executives get paid a windfall if the price does not increase or decrease. They get paid for hanging around for the stock-option vesting period, and rewarded, in dollars, for the difference in the issue price and the current price.

Holding stock options in check better protects the shareholder, period. Allowing employees to sell their company stock also protects the everyday investor, as restricting employees potentially keeps a good chunk of shares off the market. This only becomes a factor when the participants hold a significant percentage of the shares.

As key influencers with our clients and within our industry, it is up to us to think of the plan participants first. Let's ask the tough questions and use our influence in the industry to do what is right for the plan participants. Very few firms routinely review clients to see if they meet their business standards (ultimately an ethics question). I would rather be truthful in the sales process and lose the business, than do whatever it takes to win the business and try to do the right thing later. If we all start practicing the common sense approach in the sales process, the plan participants will win, without the intervention of our government. In the long run, sound business ethics and common sense will pay off.

CHAPTER VIII

Successful Conversion Management

First Impressions Do Count

As in any business, we all get one chance at making first impressions. In the sales process, the service providers get one opportunity to present their value proposition, and then one opportunity to follow-up and execute a conversion as promised. As a plan sponsor, you only get one opportunity with your participants. Any slip-ups can hurt your credibility.

For record-keeping service providers or brokers, it is crucial that you meet these expectations initially, because if you don't, there will always be doubt. Believe it or not, you will have more latitude for errors if you perform a flawless conversion, than you will if you botch up the conversion. Simply stated, it comes to down to an initial first experience. It is far easier to enjoy a long-lasting and rewarding relationship when the process starts off well, and you will build a lot of goodwill. By starting off poorly, you will most likely create doubt for the lifetime of the relationship, or at least as long your current client contacts are around.

This is why I advise firms to celebrate new business only after the plan has been successfully implemented, not when it is awarded. Complacency is not a characteristic of success. Therefore, it is crucial that the first impression you make is a good one.

Mistakes to Avoid

This is where brokers and investment advisors have to pay attention. Your role is to support the record-keeping service provider, not to get the assets moved over as quickly as possible. With record-keeping service providers, the key to success is managing the process on an ongoing basis, down to the smallest detail.

Major mistakes to avoid in the conversion process:

1. Not managing by dates/no conversion schedule (*Many firms issue a conversion schedule in the sales process, but that is the last time anyone references it.*)

2. Not paying attention to the details (*participant communication, investment fund issues, plan document issues, etc.*)

3. Dumping surprise work on the client, with massive paperwork that is hard to understand (*In other words, dead opposite of the sales pitch which claimed there would not be much work in the conversion, or ongoing process, for the plan sponsor.*)

4. No communication with the firm that is losing the business, such as the firm liquidating the assets or the prior record keeper (*It is very difficult to perform a conversion without their involvement.*)

5. Not doing your homework in the sales process, which leads to false promises, or bad information, including:
   - Contingent Deferred Sales Charges (CDSCs) being charged
   - Prior record keeper having a 60- or 90-day notification window
   - Prior record keeper having reconciliation issues (tying the assets to the records)
   - Certain funds can't be liquidated
   - Prototype document sold not retaining all of the rights and features of the previous document (*This is a major no-no.*)
   - Prior record keeper not valuing the plan as of the effective conversion date

6. Having monies not invested appropriately at the effective conversion date. (*This is where the write-offs occur!*)

Managing the Process

To have a successful conversion process means you must manage the process from the start, within days of being awarded the business. Use the *right to left* conversion process, whereby you pick a conversion date, with plenty of lead-time, and manage all interim dates. You would be surprised how many firms start off on the wrong foot because the assigned conversion manager is too swamped with work, or no one starts to think about the conversion process until it is close to panic time. This can be avoided by following a three-step process:

1. Create a kick-off meeting within one week after being awarded the business. Include all parties involved in the conversion process: record keeper, consultant, advisor, directed trustee, client, etc. Let everyone know in advance that the agenda is to walk through the conversion process, assign roles and responsibilities, and agree to realistic conversion dates. Make sure the previous record keeper, directed trustee, etc., are informed and included in the process early on, as you don't want any surprises down the road. This is setting the tone the right way.

2. Set-up a weekly meeting to discuss the status of the conversion. The lead account manager (generally the record keeper) should send the updated conversion schedule showing completed tasks and agenda, and highlighting any issues necessary for discussion. I have yet to hear a client, consultant, or investment advisor complain of having too much information during the conversion process.

3. Create a user manual for the client that clearly identifies the process during the conversion and afterward. This user manual should provide the client with an overview of the yearly timing of deliverables, including: participant statements, payroll processing, compliance testing, distribution processing, etc. The manual also provides the client with any forms they may need to complete and information on how to deliver or exchange data.

Customize the Details of the Conversion Up Front

Each client is different; so take the time to customize the details of the conversion up front. A majority of the process is the same, but the investment process and communication process will be different. Many companies try to streamline the process by issuing generic conversion steps, in a left-to-right format, listing how long each process should take, not taking into account that they are not managing to a specific deadline, or that each client is unique.

When drop-dead dates are issued in a right-to-left approach, if certain key tasks are not completed on time, the effective conversion date is in jeopardy. No one wants this to happen, especially after informing the participants of the change.

It is equally important to empower one person to lead the charge, with everyone flowing through that person with questions, comments, and issues. This process is most successful when all parties are actively involved in the process through frequent updates via conference calls and e-mail.

Whether you are the attorney, custodian, record keeper, investment advisor, communication specialist, etc., it is crucial that everyone is on the same page. If you are an advisor or consultant, it is generally a good rule of thumb to give firms one chance in the conversion process, and if they are not proactive, do not recommend them in the future. Why should anyone go with these firms, as it is a major risk, especially on investing the funds in a timely manner. A wise industry consultant once said, "If you want to take risks, go to Las Vegas, but don't do it with plan sponsors and the participants' money."

Focus on the Investments and Participant Communications

It is essential to focus on the investments and participant communications. As we all know, most people don't like change; therefore, it is just as important to manage participants' expectations. From an investment perspective, participants should never be out of the market just because the plan sponsor decided to change record-keeping service providers. Regulations dictate if the participants will not have access to their accounts for over three days, then the plan sponsor must inform the participants of the blackout period (why and how long). This notice must be provided at least 30 days in advance of the blackout period.

Furthermore, it is critical that the record-keeping service provider, advisor, or consultant does not make a back-door investment decision on behalf of the participants, simply by stating that the monies will be invested in a money-market fund or Stable-Value Fund during the conversion. Yes, this is an investment decision, one that record keepers or advisors inadvertently make every day without understanding the ramifications. Many understand the errors of their ways after the fact, generally with a big fat check they must write to the plan.

Out-of-the-market means their monies are not invested in a manner similar to their pre-conversion investment objectives, and that all converted monies are invested in a money market or Stable Value Fund for 1-60 days while the new record keeper completes the conversion. This is a recipe for disaster, as no person can defend this action, even in the age of daily-to-daily conversions.

Provide the Choice of Mapping or Estimating During the Conversion

Instead, a plan sponsor should be provided the following choices during the conversion:

1. **Mapping** — This process maps the funds from the prior investment menu into "like" funds in the current menu. Simply stated, the monies will not be out of the market for more than one day, and all participants' monies are invested per their long-term asset-allocation decisions made with the prior record keeper.

2. **Estimating** — This process collects investment elections from all participants for the converted monies and/or ongoing contributions, using the new investment menu in the month preceding the effective conversion date. On that date, all monies are estimated into the funds, based on the prior record keeper's most recent balance (as close to the conversion date as possible). The monies are reconciled upon completion of the conversion process.

Both processes keep all monies in the market, but the estimation process has two downfalls. If the participants do not make an election, the monies are generally estimated into a default fund such as a Stable-Value Fund. The other is that terminated participants are hard to track down, and it is important no one makes an investment decision on behalf of these participants.

In Review

- Raise the red flag if you are a plan sponsor, or investment advisor, and do not have a conversion schedule that clearly articulates the roles and responsibilities and all deadlines.
- The good record-keeping service providers proactively manage the process with weekly e-mails and conference calls.
- If you are the directed trustee or custodian, it is crucial that you get required documents from all parties in advance of the conversion date, as well as send out a daily e-mail to all parties after the effective conversion date letting them know where the monies are invested. Never go a day without letting the record keeper or plan sponsor know about un-invested cash.

- If you are an investment advisor and the process does not seem to be going well, it is imperative you stick to the conversion schedule and manage the process. In the interim, you might want to have a chat with the person who runs the record-keeping division, and explain that the current process is inadequate. If he or she can't show you a standard process that works, do not use the firm again, as the disorganization will lead to ongoing issues.

CHAPTER IX

Participant Communications Planning

ommunications is a crucial component in selecting your record-keeping service provider and advisor/consultants. The most important decision regarding communications is to choose the best campaign for your participants and budget, ranging from prototype to custom packages. Regardless of the route the communication plan takes, it is essential that the campaign cover:

- Benefits of a retirement plan or plans (include all information about other plans, as well as defined-benefit plans)
- Personalizing the retirement goal on a participant level
- Long-term investment strategies
- Your plan specifics (e.g., loans and company matches)
- Your investment fund selections and objectives
- How to use the Interactive Voice Response (IVR) and Internet systems
- Exit communications (termination information, including rollover features)

Participant communications spawned a whole new breed of companies, focused solely on developing communications directed at the plan-sponsor level. In fact, many of the top service providers created units for supporting customized participant communications, including on-site presentations.

As in all businesses, the higher the level of customization, the greater the prices to the plan sponsor. In addition, the higher the assets in your plan, the more leverage you have related to customized participant communication campaigns and on-site participant meetings.

With the advent of Internet technology, record-keeping service providers can deliver more customization. With increased technology, many of the companies that built their business plan around participant communications have been sold or merged with other complementary companies.

Communication Material Selection

Each service provider will offer some combination of retirement disks, Internet, CDs, videos and paper communications. It is essential for you to review the prototype communications of all service providers, to determine if they apply to your employees, since every company has a different culture and philosophy.

On-site enrollment meetings are costly to the plan sponsor, especially if they take place during the workday. It is essential that all on-site meetings are substantive and entertaining, especially any on-site meetings after the first year.

Ironically, one of the greatest complaints I hear from plan sponsors is that during the first year participant communications are great, but after that the meetings and materials are close to non-existent.

Communication Strategy

Always ask your potential service providers, during the selection process, to spend time discussing their communication campaign for your employees. Make sure you understand all of the costs. Some companies will include live employee sessions that sound great, but you must find out what the agenda will be and how it applies to your situation. In addition, many service providers offer customized communications that allow you to tailor the materials to include your logo, company colors, investment selections, and to potentially interject your philosophy. Remember, there are three phases of the communication campaign: Initial, Ongoing, and Exit.

Communication Process Review

Ongoing communication is often overlooked during the service-provider search. The most important components for ongoing communication are the traditional participant statement and daily Internet statement. Both should provide financial information in a format that is easy to read. Ask for specific examples of the participant statement(s) currently utilized by the service provider for plans of similar size, both over the Internet and on paper. Check for color, design, and variance among the statement samples. The majority of service providers will allow you to moderately customize your participant statement, but do not be surprised if you find a "canned" approach from some providers. You should also ask for a copy of the newsletter or fund performance guide they send with the participant statements. As the Internet becomes a more prevalent information delivery platform, the participant's paper statement will be issued on a less-frequent basis, perhaps even limited to one annual statement.

The Internet is also an excellent way to deliver plan information; therefore, it is crucial to leverage the Internet. In today's society, Internet access is available at the library, grocery store, etc.; therefore, do not minimize the Internet as an effective tool.

Participants want one site and one statement for all of their employee benefits. The service providers who can accommodate this, will win in the long run.

Company Culture

Select the communication tools your participants would use. Videos or CDs often sound and look great when you review them, but make sure your audience would enjoy them. A communication planning session is essential in order to understand your culture and philosophy before your selected service provider begins the communication campaign. For service providers that offer custom communications, ask if you can get involved in the editing or writing in order to decrease the cost. In addition, ask for specific client communication campaigns as examples. We recommend utilizing the prototype IVR brochures/wallet cards, investment fund sheets (from the mutual-fund companies or broker), and prototype long-term investment planning guides. In addition, we recommend they first log-on to the site and perform a demonstration that highlights the investment election process, using retirement modeling, and asset-allocation software tools. You can customize your communications with a cover letter highlighting your plan features, how you selected the investment funds, and, potentially, the service provider. On-site meetings may be an option, depending on the planning session and cost of meeting (soft and hard dollars).

Companies often request one-on-one counseling for their participants. We believe this is a positive trend that can be accomplished by interactive technology, or direct meetings with registered investment advisors.

Bottom Line*: Can the employee easily determine, at any time, the amount to save, in order to reach his/her realistic retirement goals?*

On-Site Presentations

Plan sponsors that hire a record-keeping service provider to conduct live presentations often do not know, nor interview, the person who will perform these sessions. This is a crucial step, as you want to select a person that will relate to your audience.

It is also crucial that the presenter is in the correct attire, as the person wearing a suit in a casual business environment may not be accepted. In addition, select a location that is cozy for all, and is conducive to a Q&A session, as well as an area for one-on-one questions in private. The location should also have Internet access and the appropriate AV hardware.

Foreign Languages

Plan sponsors should manage expectations within their organization and with their service providers based on the cost/benefits of their company demographics. Recordkeeping Service Providers that provide foreign language services via the website, Call Center, and paper communications can not provide this service at the same standard costs as compared to a company that provides the exact same services to an all English company. Simply stated, it costs more to provide these services.

Having worked with many companies with significant numbers of employees speaking a foreign language, we have found that the key to success is not just providing the above standard services, but understanding the dialect. Therefore it is important to work with the HR person who can translate appropriately, as the standard off the shelf communications in their foreign language might miss the point.

If foreign language services are a high priority, make sure you actually test the service providers solutions, from strategy through actual services. Some service providers offer a Call Center approach whereby all inquiries and transactions are handled through a customer service representative. It is important to found out how many customer service representatives speak the language, as if it is only one or two representatives, you may have queue or absence issues. The best companies have offshore Call Center solutions to supplement their Call Centers in the states, to ensure a 24/7 solution. If the solution is web-based or IVR, test it, to make sure the solution will work for you company.

Bottom Line: *Plan sponsors must be prepared to pay more for these services. For larger companies, we recommend leveraging your internal HR staff for onsite and custom participant communications.*

CHAPTER X

Building a Successful Record-Keeping Business

The Daily Grind

Athletes and coaches understand that it is easy for anyone watching a game to second-guess a player, manager, coach, or referee after the action is over. The same is true in the world of defined-contribution administration, whereby record-keeping administrators perform hundreds of transactions each day. The similarity between sports and record-keeping administration is that the critics often don't understand the details of the game or process, nor the fast-paced environment in which the players and administrators work.

Mistakes Happen

No matter how many controls are in place, some errors will occur, and we all hope they do not have an impact on the financial bottom line or to the client. When an error occurs, you must act quickly, ethically and diligently. Those who have never been involved in record-keeping administration are often heard to make comments such as, "It's simple bookkeeping; how can you make an error like that?" If you are a record-keeping service provider, invite that person to join your staff for a week and actually perform the job!

As record-keeping administrators, we all know of the client that seems "cursed." You've made one big error, or a few small ones, and the client tells you that if there's another error you are gone. Well, you can bet the house that the next error is going to happen on that account, even with added proof and controls.

I recall a certain plan for which we processed payroll contributions semi-monthly in a quarterly valuation environment (meaning we ran contribution runs during the quarter, by purchasing shares during the quarter). The contribution information was sent by tape and hardcopy, along with a check. The first input tape totaling $10,000 matched the check. Next pay period, everything matched again, but totaled $20,000. By the third payroll, the amount was $30,000. Unfortunately, the payroll company had made the error of sending "cumulative" tapes and the company erred by sending checks matching the totals. So we received an irate phone call saying that we were terrible record keepers. All of our proof and controls had worked perfectly, but we hadn't asked the record keeper or manager to perform a common-sense test to see if the total contribution made sense. In this case, the payroll company made an error by sending cumulative tapes, and the company erred by sending the matching checks. Of course, when we had to liquidate the purchased shares, we were short money, which we, as the record keeper, had to pay. Was it really the record keeper's fault?

People Skills

This business is not easy, because in order to be successful, you must have the following traits:

- Common sense
- Mathematical inclination (and enjoy numbers)
- Enjoy working in a repetitive environment
- Strong organizational skills
- Enjoy reading legal code
- Enjoy working with people (at least most of the jobs require this trait)

In fact, these are almost the same criteria for anyone in a plan sponsor's Human Resources department. Yet as the demanding field of record-keeping administration and Employee Benefits continues to grow, still no universities or colleges have a degree program to better train future EB specialists (or weed them out).

As a record keeper, your work is showcased every day on the Internet. No longer do participants have to wait for their quarterly statements to find out how their investment funds are doing. Record-keeping administrators have to post transactions accurately, and timely, every day. Attorneys and consultants see their work posted on the Internet; no longer do the participants have to beg and plead for an SPD (summary plan description) or plan document. In today's environment, there is less pressure at participant statement time, as the participants are no longer waiting for information.

The Downside

So, why "eat nails for breakfast?" Because most record-keeping service providers are probably understaffed. One computer glitch or inaccurate trade can throw off a reconciliation for a plan or plans, and there goes the perfectly planned day. The more efficient you become, the more work you get assigned from your managers. In this business, managers quickly find the go-getters and move their most important and critical work to these people. It is truly a conundrum for the eager, aggressive and good record- keeping administrator. In fact, many record-keeping service companies expect even the managers to perform day-to-day work. This is the worst thing they could do, as managers are needed to manage the process flow.

Back in 1986, when record-keeping administration was just in its infancy, plans were processed quarterly or annually, and record keepers were able to achieve profits of 60%. Today, many record-keeping service providers struggle to break even on daily valuation plans. Those that are breaking even have found a solution, which is simply to price each client to make money. "Eating nails for breakfast" means performing 100% error-free every day, while making a profit with no write-offs. Anything less is unacceptable.

In the record-keeping administration world, the key to success is streamlining the process with the perfect amount of proof and controls. Too many proof and controls, and you dip into the profits. Not enough proof and controls, and your errors increase which means rework and potential write-offs. Virtually every record-keeping service provider has a different methodology, and what's worse, companies with multiple sites often have different environments, systems, and proof and controls at each site. Once you start down the path of inefficiency within a company, it is hard to reign in. If you try to fix it, you risk losing clients in the short-term, due to the conversions or upgrades.

The Building Blocks: Marketing and Service Strategy

The Marketing Strategy is the lifeblood of your organization, and the keys to success are these:

- Become a marketing-oriented firm
- Know your service strategy
- Constantly eliminate old-school processes

In the real world, it seems most managers cannot distinguish between marketing and sales. Sales is a component of marketing.

Marketing Strategy

Then, what is a marketing-oriented firm? The characteristics are straightforward:

- **Customer Focused** — They know their marketplace and customers well. A lot of firms claim they know this well, but if they did, they would be more profitable today. The best firms know the distribution channels that work for them, and do not stray. They understand their clients' needs and wants, and what makes them select a service provider. Your firm is not customer focused if you are constantly making excuses about why you lost current business, or lost to another firm in a recent bidding process. Saying you lost to another firm, simply because of fees, is only an excuse. The best firms understand their prospects and clients and deliver an honest, straightforward message. It is almost to the point of not caring about their competitors, because they know they are the best.

- **Goal Focused** — A firm that is willing to set goals is one that is honest with its performance and clients. Simply review the converse: If a firm does not have goals related to revenues, operational efficiency, or implementing new technologies, it is one that will be complacent. Technically, these firms are less than complacent. It is crucial that all managers work together to set, and manage to, goals. A firm without goals is a firm without service standards.

- **One Firm/One Team** — When the entire company and team is focused on the same goal, there is no doubt the clients are happier, as is the company team. If one person is not on the same page, it is virtually impossible to reach the highest goals. The higher the position of that person, or persons, means the greater impact they will have on the positive or negative approach to the client.

Ironically, most businesses think they are all of the above, but what I have found in consulting engagements is that most senior managers are unrealistic about how the marketplace perceives them. This is why revenue, growth, and profitability goals are not met.

Turn this around today by embarking on a marketing strategic-planning process that you set as your priority. Don't skip the meetings because you have too much work to do. By having the meetings, the work will be better managed in the future. Here is what you should do:

Step 1: Set aside 2-3 days for an initial on-site strategy meeting. The agenda should be:

- Complete a marketing check-up that assesses the following components:

  Internal Analysis — Is your entire company on the same page? Are your leaders setting the tone? Are you setting aggressive goals and measuring to them? Are you rewarding employees and senior managers for enacting change or setting high goals? Is your internal culture what you want?

  External Analysis — Where do you stand in the scheme of market share for your target market? Review the state of the market and economy. How does the marketplace perceive you?

  Identify Action Steps — What do you need to do operationally to win more business? What do you need to do from a marketing perspective to get your message to your target market?

  Review — Look at your PR, advertising, pricing, and strategic partnerships

- Create your marketing plan.
- Set quarterly meeting dates for the next year.

Step 2: Incorporate your marketing strategy as part of every management meeting.

Step 3: Measure your progress, and be honest.

Service Strategy

One of the most important functions when performing your internal analysis is identifying your value proposition or your service strategy. In fact, after reading thousands of RFPs and listening to thousands of presentations, it seems many firms are proclaiming all three hallmarks of service listed below.

It is essential that each firm recognize their strategy. It can only be one of the following three approaches. (The book, *The Discipline of Market Leaders*, provides an in-depth look at these approaches.)

1. **Low-Cost Service Provider** — These firms are the most operationally efficient, and the reason they can charge low fees is that they do not accept plans that do not fit their process. The best low-cost service providers lag the technology trend by 12 – 18 months; however, when it is implemented, it is well tested.

2. **Technology Leader** — These firms are always adding innovations or promising them at rapid pace. Not all of the technologies work, but their clients know that they will get the latest in technology.

3. **Premium Service Provider** — These firms charge the highest fees and have the highest flexibility for serving plans. Generally these firms adopt technology 6 – 12 months after it is tried and tested.

If you are a plan sponsor, consultant, or investment advisor you should immediately throw out a company that proclaims to be all three. If any one firm were truly all three, they would have close to 100% of the business. From a plan sponsor's perspective, it is important to pick the type of firm you want to work with. In our industry, the low-cost providers often get a bad rap because they are not flexible. What has really happened is the plan sponsor (or investment advisor) went the low-cost route with the wrong expectations. Soon, the plan sponsor is complaining that they are not getting premium service, and the low-cost provider is blamed.

Therefore, the most important step for the record-keeping service provider is to select a strategy and stick with it.

Marketing Pitfalls

Let's review some of the most common mistakes record-keeping service providers make in the marketing strategy process:

- Pricing to market, as opposed to pricing based on your costs
- Over-promising deliverables or technology; saying 'yes' to ad-hoc tasks during the sales process; or taking on additional ongoing tasks without charging
- Not budgeting for technology costs (software and hardware)
- Not managing the employee turnover efficiently
- Trying to play the volume game (this is a common mistake)
- Failure to include service contracts outlining responsibilities, hence, by default, the record keeper is responsible for everything
- Taking on business that is not an area of expertise, such as a 403(b), when the rest of the business is all 401(k) and profit sharing
- Placing your resources on those that yell the loudest or are unprofitable
- Thinking the small-plan marketplace (the untapped market) is the solution
- Wasting valuable resources on RFPs that you have little chance of winning (a long-winded way of saying validate your leads appropriately)
- Falling for the old "If you do this one for me well at low prices, there will be a lot more business down the road" hustle

How do you overcome these obstacles? Whether you are a new company or an experienced firm, it is essential to follow all of these recommendations:

- Understand all of your costs, and build in a buffer for technology, write-offs, and direct plan expenses (travel, printing, postage).
- Know your pricing schedule and don't lower it just to win a sale.
- Build the cost of conversion of the plans into the overall cost.
- Know and work your target market and distribution channels.
- Eliminate unprofitable plans, ASAP.

Eliminating unprofitable plans is easy to say, but hard to do, especially if the record-keeping service is not the core of the firm. If you are a record-keeping service provider as a core business, simply visit with the plan sponsor and/or controlling entity (a broker, advisor, consultant, or other party) and let them know you are not making money on the relationship, and need to do one or more of the following:

- Increase the fees (this can be graduated).
- Change the process flow to reduce costs and increase profitability.
- Eliminate, or outsource, a portion of the process (such as compliance testing or Form 5500 completion).
- Negotiate with another provider to perform the work at the same cost to the client, where you retain 5% or 10% of the fees.
- End the relationship. (We have all experienced the difficult client, and in many cases, it is just better to move on.)

If you are part of a larger organization, and the larger organization does not want to put the whole relationship at risk, then you must renegotiate your new pricing schedule internally (unless you are a true cost center, which is very rare nowadays). You can let another department yell and scream that they incorporated the fees you told them. Although they may be correct, that is still not a reason to continue to perform the work at a loss, as it will negatively affect the organization's bottom line.

The same strategy works with your internal firm as it would with an outside advisor; it simply does not help this client, or any of your other clients, to continue to operate at a deficit. To hire and retain the best people and technology requires capital, which is best derived from profits.

The Business Plan/Business Strategy

The best way to manage your business, partners, shareholders (if applicable) and team is to create a business plan and manage by it. I credit Dr. Bill Boulton of Auburn University for the format I use today with clients. This is complementary to the marketing strategy process. The business plan must include the following:

- **Business Strategy**
- **Industry Analysis** — Know you products and services from an industry perspective (not your perspective). It is crucial to understand the

infrastructure of the industry as well as the key success factors for the industry such as:
- Customer Segments
- Competitors and their strategies
- Suppliers
- Barriers to Entry
- Substitution to Products (for example the current TPA Model can be replaced by the ASP Model)

- **Industry Trends** — Look 3-5 years out, not just the marketplace today.
- **Business Strategy Analysis** — Your strategic goals and business strategy. The strategy breaks down to all functions necessary for success (marketing, sales, and operations), and sets financial goals (including market share, profitability, and stock price if applicable) . Make sure you know the industry standards for integration of systems. Know your resource requirements and dependencies on suppliers/systems.
- **SWOT Analysis** (Strengths, Weaknesses, Opportunities, and Threats)
- **Human Resource Plan**
- **Compensation Plan**
- **Job Descriptions**
- **Hiring Strategy**
- **Training Plan**
- **Operation Plan** (detailed to complement the Business Strategy)
- **Defined Process Flow**
- **Resources Needed**
- **Proof and Controls Necessary**
- **Supplier/Partner Negotiation**
- **Disaster Recovery**
- **Risk Analysis**
- **Quality Standards/Measurement**
- **Space/Location**
- **Technology Plan**

If you want to get an honest assessment of your company, create an Advisory or Review Board. This is where you will receive sound advice, especially advice you may not agree with. Your Advisory Board should include:

- Top managers within your company or group
- 1-2 distribution channels (A consultant or advisor)
- 1-2 business leaders in the community

It is crucial that you do not put together a board of like people, who all think the same way, or will simply agree with everything you have to say. The best Advisory Boards focus on the top issues to serve your clients, profitability, and overall business plan. It is imperative the board stays focused on the major sections of the business plan, and not micro issues. Don't avoid the tough discussions, as this will not help you or your firm in the short or long run. Do not fall into the trap of writing a business plan for yourself or your firm without in-depth discussion, as this does no good. Also, the worst thing you can do is throw away the business plan when your plan goes sour. This is when you really need to focus on revamping the business plan and using your Advisory Board to ensure you are on track. Do not be afraid of failure, because if you don't try something, it is hard to succeed in new avenues. By setting your advisory board up in this manner, not only will you get good advice, but you will also have passionate spokespersons for your business.

Value Proposition

Each and every person at your company should be able to state your value proposition in less than 2 minutes. In many companies I visit, only the sales staff and senior management know the value proposition, and often it is a memorized statement, recited just to win business. If the value proposition is well known, it will permeate to vendors, clients, friends, etc. Your best salespersons are the very people who talk to the clients each and every day. As discussed in the Marketing Strategy, know your strengths and make sure everyone believes in them.

Your value proposition must be consistent and something everybody believes in. If you are a record-keeping service provider, your value proposition may be one of these:

- Flexibility of investment selection and plan design, at a fair price
- Low, or no, fees with all of the flexibility you need
- A premium service provider that provides the personal touch at all levels: the plan sponsor, participant, and partners
- Record-keeping administration that works every day, with an emphasis on compliance, all at a fair price that virtually eliminates unexpected costs for non-compliance

For investment advisors or brokers the value proposition may be something like:

- We take full fiduciary responsibility for the investment selection and monitoring.
- We help you design the most cost effective plan and deliver a communication campaign that works.
- We know the business and will ensure your costs will be the lowest in the industry while providing all of the bells and whistles that the large firms are receiving.

Attorneys and consultants should have only one value proposition, and that is to provide solutions (not just provide issues with no solutions).

Business Creed

Very few record-keeping service providers have a business creed, but it is one of the most important foundations you can make as an individual and company. The key to a business creed is building the foundation and living by it. The Tylenol example is the best example of living up to a creed, in my opinion, as the company did not hesitate to pull their pills off the shelves even though they had a pretty good idea that the problem was a case of tampering. In our business, the immediate response has to be to do what is right for the participant. This reaction needs to be at all levels. Don't use a business creed just for marketing purposes; do it because it is what you believe in. Most importantly, if someone in your company lies, cheats, or steals (including expense reports, copying software you have not purchased, plagiarizing for marketing and sales, etc.) you must take appropriate action; otherwise your creed means nothing. Alternatively, you can operate in an environment without a creed, or one that condones or allows plagiarizing, stealing software, etc.

Bottom line: *The senior management sets the tone and foundation, and actions speak louder than words.*

DWC Consultants has a Code of Ethics and a Creed, which can be found in Appendix 3. We must all practice what we preach, to build the foundation your employers, clients, and partners will recognize. Firms with strong ethical foundations have a strategic advantage. Don't work with firms and professionals that tolerate unethical practices.

Once setting your creed, make sure you review it quarterly.

Ultimately, if your service providers or advisors/consultants do not practice strong ethical standards, most likely you will end up with services that do not live up to expectations. As a plan sponsor, you could be left facing a serious situation such as:

1. Having to take ultimate responsibility for a non-compliance issue with a plan document, SPD, report, participant communication, etc.
2. Taking the consequences for untimely government reporting or required testing
3. Being unaware of fine-print indemnifications or limits on liability within your service contract
4. Finding hidden errors at the participant level
5. Having to make good on errors made at the participant level

Unfortunately, the best time to measure the ethical standards of your advisors and service providers is at the time of adversity. When you find firms that take responsibility immediately and honestly, hold on to them, as everyone makes mistakes. From a service provider perspective, you will be rewarded for a strong a business creed.

Marketing — Getting Your Value Proposition to the Marketplace

When looking for new business, record-keeping service providers can target companies based on size, assets, industry, region, and plan type. Furthermore, they can target plans directly, professional organizations, the broker community, investment advisors, and other industry service organizations as well.

This targeted marketing needs to tie into the value proposition. Review your current book of business to determine trends and similarities, and highlight your most profitable clients. In addition, review the quality surveys (to be discussed later in the chapter), to determine trends and similarities, on both ends of the quality score spectrum. This will allow you to better leverage these firms as references, but most importantly, these firms are most likely saying good things about you in their circles. In the defined-contribution business, it seems everyone knows everyone, and we all run into each other at conferences, various industry organizations, and in the sales process. As we all know, a negative service relationship results in one client telling eight more people about the poor services, and so on, and so on. Word of mouth is still a valuable marketing tool!

Bottom Line: *Know your strengths and capitalize on them.*

Marketing mistakes you will want to avoid:

- Sending the wrong target message, as this may alienate your prospect or targeted distribution channel
- Targeting a larger marketplace than your current book (This will result in a lot of effort on the sales side with no results, as you will not be able to back it up with references or facts.)
- Wasting dollars on brochures, trips, etc.
- Targeting the wrong channels or size of business (This may send a message to your true marketplace that you do not covet your current clients.)
- Creating a message that your firm is all things to all people (This may work for large service providers.)
- Having no value proposition on any marketing materials, web or print
- Deviating from the region you can effectively cover
- Name dropping; it will backfire (using partners as leverage to win business, such as accounting firms, directed trustees, mutual fund companies, consultants, etc.)

Finally, make sure you budget accordingly for marketing and sales. Marketing is getting your value proposition to your target market and branding your company. Sales is the act of engaging with a prospect in an effort to win business. On that note, make sure everything related to marketing is correct and designed to serve your target marketplace. Consider the following:

1. A catchy name, especially if you use the names of two or more partners (Don't be afraid to keep the formal name, but use a catchy phrase that builds off of the names. Record-keeping firms should not sound like law firms.)
2. Hire a designer to create logos or enhance your current logo (All successful companies change their logo over time and use them to revitalize their marketing campaigns and their internal teams.)

3. Leverage your website for the marketing message and make sure it stays up to date (no bad links or outdated messages)

4. Leverage all e-mails sent to prospects with signatures that incorporate logos for linking to your website.

5. Write and submit articles to appropriate Employee Benefit journals.

6. Sponsoring Trade Shows—These can pay off, but never sponsor a trade show without attending the previous year or quarter. (Sales people will tell you that a booth is well worth it, but, in reality, at many shows booths receive little traffic and the target market is not as promised. If you do take a booth, make sure it is continuously attended, and that you hand out material only to prospects.)

7. Advertising—If you choose to go this route, ask your clients, distribution channels, and partners what journals they read (as this will most likely match your target market). Before selecting advertising mediums, ask the following:
   • Their circulation statistics and target market
   • If any of your competitors are advertising in the same issue
   • What the cover story and content is for the issue in which you will be advertising (as you do not want to have your advertisement in an issue that your target market might find controversial or that actually criticizes your approach)
   • A list of repeat advertising buyers
   • References (call them to ask the return on investment)

8. Donate time and money to your community and good causes

I hate putting the donation and community work under marketing, because your company should do what they want to, not to reap marketing benefits. If you do this because your heart is in the right place, it is marketing at its best.

Your Competitors — A Key Component of the External Marketing Strategy

From a marketing campaign perspective, it is best to say your competitors are the recognizable national names in the industry, or the favorite local or regional firms. However, in order to increase sales and ensure the back door is closed, make sure you know who your competitors really are. Everybody eventually goes up against everybody, but the purpose of this drill is to know whom your top 3-5 competitors are. Once identified, it is crucial to understand their value propositions, marketing campaigns, distribution channels, etc. For example, the major automakers buy the cars of their competitors and break them down to find their latest innovations and design; so, there is no reason not to perform your own research analysis.

Research can be handled by hiring a research firm, or through interviews of employee prospects and potential strategic partners. The latter is often the best approach, as the interviews can be turned into a marketing opportunity. Do not ask your interviewees to send you proprietary or confidential information. Rather, at the end of the interview, ask them if your value proposition is competitive, and if there are any weaknesses. If you are interviewing or meeting with potential strategic partners, NEVER tell them you will give them business, if they send you business. Always win business on your merits!

Use your market knowledge to better build your service and attack your weaknesses. Most importantly, don't alter your price because you find out your fees are too high, as your competitors may be buying business (don't assume they are efficient). If you know you are at maximum efficiency, and are offering a compelling service option, don't be afraid to lose business based on price.

Pricing Strategy/Profit Margins

It is easy to say revenues must exceed costs. It is also easy for a consultant to visit a record-keeping service provider and say, "Your problem is your fees are too low and your process is inefficient." Thanks a lot for the advice, and how much am I paying you for that revelation? You must improve the process from an efficiency perspective and set appropriate pricing.

Record-keeping service providers must eliminate all plans that are not profitable. In fact, you should take this one step further; eliminate all plans that do not reach your after-tax profitability goals. Making one cent on a $35,000 year-long investment is not a good return, nor would any sane person put money in a bank in the hopes of returning one penny.

When performing this analysis, you may be thinking that you can't raise your fees, because you will not be competitive. Technically, you already are not competitive if that is the case, depending on your approach (low-cost or premium-service provider). If the plan is unprofitable, it is; and that is the problem you need to solve. Don't worry about the competition in these cases, because if your pricing strategy is based on them and you are losing money, how much longer are you really going to be in business?

Therefore, your pricing strategy needs to follow these steps:

1. If you employ a salesperson, sales compensation must be built into cost grades

2. Determine your costs in the current environment
   - Accounting and consulting firms track time, which is the best way to track profitability if everyone completes their time cards accurately (the more detailed you can be, by type of activity, the better, especially segregating record-keeping administration, rework, conversion, and compliance).
   - If you are not using the time-recording method, use a financial-analysis software program that allows you to estimate costs based on managers input (often by FTE or estimated time spent on each plan).
   - Eliminate politics when allocating overhead and shared costs.
   - Eliminate continued excuses for accounts that are not profitable. (Managers often justify their numbers by blaming — such as having too many new people, or recent account acquisitions, etc.)
   - Make sure all costs and expenses for each plan add up to the total costs.
   - Allocate all revenue sharing to the appropriate account.
   - Determine how to handle one-time write-offs. (If a plan has write-offs in consecutive years, consider the true reasons.)

3. Estimate your costs, if you change your operations to reduce costs on at-risk plans. (You must include implementation and training costs.)

4. Determine if you can charge for perceived ancillary services, such as compliance work.

5. Create a report that lists all plans that exceed 40% gross margins, 20% gross margins, zero, and all that are in the red (list plans in their first year separately).

Let's focus on the ancillary services. Plan sponsors like a one-price, all-inclusive package, but if your pricing strategy does not include costs of all services and you are not making money, then this approach is invalid. Regardless of your pricing approach — *a la carte* or bundled — internally price everything in the bidding process and in your annual review!

The marketplace will pay a premium for the following:

- Compliance services (plan design, document creation, and all required testing)
- Form 5500 completion
- Re-runs due to client error (Very few firms charge this; but if you have to perform the work twice, why give it away?)
- Fees that can be charged to the participant (although these may not be the best approach in the long run, such as loan fees)

As discussed earlier, the fact that the plan sponsor is not paying out of pocket does not necessarily translate to lower fees. In fact in most cases, the participant ends up bearing the burden.

Therefore, your pricing strategy needs to be combined with your value proposition and marketing message. There is more than one way to price record-keeping administration services, regardless if the fees are charged to the plan (participants pay) or the plan sponsor pays for it out of pocket. The plan sponsor will see fee schedules in the following manner:

1. **Fully Disclosed Method** — Service provider fees are disclosed, all inclusive or *a la carte*
   - Per transaction and participant and/or
   - Asset-based fees
   - All revenue sharing is used to offset the fees.

2. **Partially Disclosed Method**—Same as above, with the exception being that revenue sharing is taken into account when bidding the services

3. **No Disclosure**—No fees are disclosed or charged and the entire record-keeping fee is paid or subsidized by the investment managers

4. **Combination** of the above

When bidding on a plan, it is crucial to outline all roles and responsibilities.

The days of a record-keeping service provider doing everything are long gone. This is true not only from a profitability standpoint, but also from a liability perspective. The record-keeping service provider is the entity with the most risk, and therefore it is important to have a straightforward contract outlining all roles, responsibilities, and timing. The service contract also should discuss the appropriate liability. Don't forget, several of the larger record keepers limit their liability to a multiple of their annual fee (which in some cases doesn't even come close to paying for their own errors).

Somewhere along the line, we, as an industry, have accepted and justified higher investment-fund expenses to serve the plan sponsor. As a record-keeping service provider, don't be afraid to say this in a sales presentation.

If the plan does not have a broker, or the investment advisor is a fee-for-service advisor, then make sure you are leveraging the commissions. If you do not use them, then the mutual fund retains them.

Your strategy should be straightforward:

1. Make sure that you are making money on all business within 12 months of receiving the business
2. Adopt a pricing strategy and stick with it, ranging from full disclosure of all fees, to one-price-fits-all (including indicating no fees out of pocket).

There is no magic bullet pricing solution that wins every time. However, disclosing all fees will eliminate any perceived improprieties in future discussions and prevent litigation related from non-disclosure.

Sales Plan

Most firms do not have a sales plan. It is crucial to resolve three issues:

1. Who is responsible for sales?
- Dedicated sales staff
- Senior managers
- Account managers

2. Who is your target for sales?
- Plan sponsors directly
- Investment advisors/brokers

- Other service providers
- Other clients of the firm (if you are not a Record-Keeping Only firm)

3. What sales methods will you use?

- Cold calling
- Direct mailings
- E-mail campaigns
- Leveraging your annual client conference and firm outings (invite prospects)
- Follow-up mailings to conferences attended (internal or external)

Qualify Sales Opportunities Before Proposals Are Sent

Once sales opportunities have been identified, qualify them carefully before deciding if a proposal should be sent. This is especially true if an RFP (Request for Proposal) is required, as they are time consuming and expensive. Therefore, before making the decision to move ahead, review the following:

- If the RFP is from a consultant, have you ever won a plan through one of their searches? If you have not, make sure you know their bias.
- If the RFP is from an investment advisor, make sure they are involved in the decision-making process, rather than completing an RFP for the advisor and then having to go up against the advisor's competition.
- If the RFP is from an investment advisor, find out how many service providers they will present to the plan sponsor. If they are presenting more than one, make sure you understand their approach, for example:
  – The advisor provides an analysis of the top providers with their recommendation
  – The advisor provides an analysis and will let the plan sponsor pick
  – The advisor simply passes on the RFP's and hope one sticks
  With any of the above, it is best for the recordkeeping service provider to present direct to the prospect.
- Do you know anyone at the company or on the decision-making board? If you are partnering with someone, such as an advisor, find out why he or she received the RFP and whom he or she knows. It is not that hard to bully your way into receiving an RFP; sometimes it is easy as a phone call.

- If the RFP is coming directly from the plan sponsor, or a consultant you haven't done business with before, will you have an opportunity to talk with the plan sponsor before bidding?

I also recommend that you develop a bank of stock answers for proposals, which you can draw upon and customize, as necessary, to complete an RFP. Send completed RFPs via e-mail, if possible. Oftentimes the hardest part of the RFP is printing and binding it. Having completed many RFPs, and also performed searches, I believe the best answers are short and to the point.

Also, for non-RFP proposals, make sure you have a web-based template. For leads from investment advisors, get them in the habit of filling out plan data on your website in order to better produce a customized proposal (although most of the proposals will have the same information, with exception of specifics related to the plan and pricing).

If you are sending a RFP, make sure you have a "peer review" process in place.

Track the Sales Process

Regardless of your methods, staffing, and sales targets, it is crucial you track the sales process. Tracking the sales flow allows the record-keeping service provider and its sales team to continually improve the sales process. A lot of companies track new business using a "pipeline" approach. However, this process makes it difficult to measure where improvement is needed in the sales process. By shifting to a "funnel tracking" system, with four stages, you can more easily track the progress, identify and avert bottlenecks, and better predict expected sales.

The stages are as follows:

1. **Qualifying Period** — An opportunity has been identified and requires additional information to determine if the firm should bid on it. This process includes a high-level review to ensure it fits the target market, and is not deemed high risk (current non-compliance issues or reconciliation issues). This phase of the funnel should contain the most plans.

2. **Qualified Period** — Indicates the record-keeping service provider has decided to move forward and prepare a proposal. Typically a plan should stay in this phase for a period of 1 – 20 days. It should be very rare that a plan does not

move to the next step from this phase, which is important for tracking and determining necessary resources. If this phase is overflowing, then you may be facing production capacity issues. Also, if your close ratios are low and proposals high, then the qualifying process must be changed, as in target market, sales process, pricing, and/or from where the leads are emanating.

3. **Delivered/Decision Period** — The proposal has been completed and is waiting for a decision from the plan sponsor and/or investment advisor/broker. This process can be split up into Proposal Delivered and Presentation Delivered. Tracking is very important in this phase for three reasons:

- After a period of time, it is possible to run a straightforward or regression analysis to closely predict new business and the timing of the decision (amount of time in the funnel)
- Resource management
- Ensuring the parties responsible for closing business are following up appropriately with prospect or decision maker

The prospect should not stay in this period longer than 60 days and, on average, a decision is made within 21 days.

4. **Decision**— This is broken down into Hired and Not Hired.

Listen to Your Sales Team and Review Tracking Reports

Finally, if you employ a direct sales team, make sure they receive the appropriate incentives. Listen to your sales team, and review the tracking reports for reasons prospects are won and lost, and adapt to the marketplace. Don't let the sales team convince the senior management to lower prices to win business, unless you can become more efficient in the process, reduce services, or leverage other means, such as the investment funds.

Sales Mistakes and Best Practices

As a search consultant, I have seen over 1,000 finalist presentations, and have created the 'Top Eleven Mistakes' that you do not want to duplicate:

1. Do not spend the first 10 minutes of a presentation talking about yourself or your company.
2. If you are presenting with multiple firms, do not fail to know the names of the other presenters and act like you have worked together before.

3. Do not read from the presentations

4. Do not send in a person who is new to the business or the company (or worse yet, makes excuses for not knowing the process).

5. Do not tell the group at the beginning that you want your lost time for starting late, because you were late!

6. Do not change the fees.

7. Do not complete only half of your presentation, especially when you miss the prospects key points.

8. Do not bring 20 people and then have only one or two of those people talk (especially the salesperson, unless they really know the process).

9. Do not have the salesperson or senior person repeat what someone just said, throughout the presentation.

10. Do not deflect answers you do not know, or try to bluff.

11. Do not prepare an Internet presentation if there is a chance the site will not work (in other words if your technology has a chance to fail, don't risk it).

In other words, do the following:

1. Bring in the service team, including the person that will be performing most of the work.

2. Present your strategic advantages and value proposition in the first five minutes. Solve the prospects issues!

3. Keep introductions short and provide biographies of the presentation team on a separate brochure or in the presentation booklet.

4. Demonstrate the value to the participant through the Internet and all participant communications (let the committee touch and feel it).

5. Emphasize compliance and proof and controls.

6. Listen to questions closely and answer them directly (yes or no when possible).

7. Don't be afraid to answer that you do not know, but that will follow up within a certain time period.

8. Have fun!

Operation Flow — Efficiency and Leveraging Your Clients and Vendors

Looking back, our business has faced a rapid revolution toward better serving the participant. In the 1980s, it was forbidden for participants to talk to record keepers, and they were often rudely told they must call their Human Resources representative. Thanks to Fidelity, this changed quickly, as they employed Customer Service Representatives to handle participants' questions (in addition to transforming this business to daily valuation virtually overnight).

Today, most record-keeping service providers recognize that their ultimate client is the plan participant. If the plan participant is happy, the company sponsoring the plan is less apt to change record-keeping service providers (of course, this means the compliance services are also handled well).

With Internet technology, companies in all service sectors have found ways to involve the client in a manner that gives them more control and happiness. For example, look at the Dell Computer model. At Dell, you can order your computer online without the help of a customer service representative. How can record-keeping service providers achieve higher efficiency, while involving the customer (plan sponsor and participant)?

- **Use the Internet for quarterly participant statements.** The participants already have access to their accounts daily, hence the participant statement is not as important as it used to be. If the client wants participant statements, charge extra, or send them a file to print themselves.

- **Do not accept paper forms for any transactions except distributions.** Use the Internet, or interactive voice response system for transfers, investment election changes, new loans, and inquiries.

- **Create a prototype proposal system via the Internet.** Limit your use of paper proposals, as the time and the cost to print in color is expensive. Furthermore, your standard proposal should remain 90% the same, including the fee schedule. There is no need to involve administrators in the creation of these documents, when they can be better used serving the current clients.

- **Only accept payroll input in a format you can readily process.** In fact, several record keepers are pushing the initial scrubbing of the data back to the plan sponsor; to ensure the dollar amounts match the wire. Do not let plan sponsors send negative contributions. If they have to make an adjustment, make them document the reason and send it on a separate file. This is important at audit time.

- **Streamline the customer service representative (CSR) process.** If you offer it, make sure you have dynamic screens (on-demand screens that flow right to the customer service rep when the participant opts out, so they know exactly where the caller is during the call). If you have to ask the participant's name and password and then locate the point at which they have further questions, it will add 2-3 minutes to each call. In today's technological environment, customer service reps are not mandatory to win business, but offer a comfort zone for the participant. Therefore, if you do not have a Call Center, an alternative response mechanism needs to be set-up through call-backs and e-mails, which are not immediate feedback. The best Call Centers' CSRs have screens that tell them what to say, which is virtually the same as the Internet and interactive voice response. These operators do not know the plan intimately, and in most cases, are not fluid in advanced defined-contribution studies. Furthermore, since they cannot provide investment advice, they are in most cases providing an ease of mind. Alternatively, you can charge additional for this service in certain market segments (very large or small).

- **Leverage the Internet for participant questions, use FAQs, and set up the process for easy navigation.** This can be done in two approaches, through e-mail questions or online chat. Online chat potentially has the same issues as phone assistance, but has several advantages:
  1. You can control the chat.
  2. The customer service rep can have multiple chat sessions simultaneously.
  3. 80% of the responses will be the same and can be hard coded (which reduces liabilities caused by inaccurate responses). Hard codong means copying and pasting from a standard set of responses.
  4. Offers "push" technology, where you can push certain screens to the participant to better answer their questions

- **If you are an unbundled service provider, link with a trading partner that is 100% automated (or go direct to the NSSC in a tri-party format with a trading partner).** Do not accept anything less. Let the directed trustee work for you and in a format and process that is easy for you. You should not be forced to use another pricing service or Internet site to download prices within one to two hours of market close. In addition, make sure the fund trust-to-records reconciliation process is automated. From a proof and control perspective, if you had to choose just one proof and control to perform each day, this should be it. (The close second would be ensuring that the reported earnings of mutual funds match your paper participant statements, and is discussed later in the chapter.) Without this automation, it will take up to 3-5 times longer to go back and reconcile issues and will most likely result in an increased number of write-offs. Don't use ad-hoc links just to win one piece of business. Also, it might be worth it to pay 1-3 basis points more for a 100% automated process (or what is commonly known as straight-through processing).

- **Participant Communications** — If you provide this service, make sure you use people who are not involved in the day-to-day record keeping for creating the materials or performing the on-site visits. Leverage the Internet, mutual-fund providers, and advisors, and charge for customized communications and printing. In today's environment, more participants want to review on their own time, so the more information you can put on the website, the better. Also, leverage CD- ROM technology allowing you to deliver your message in a method that does not take time away from peoples' jobs and is enjoyable to watch, as most people appreciate this technology.

- **Leverage your website for standard marketing and general proposal requests.** It is far less costly to maintain a website and keep it up to date, than it is to keep up paper brochures and mail them.

- **Send plan-sponsor reports by e-mail and CD-ROM**, or better yet, provide a report writer that allows plan sponsors and auditors to create their own reports. This eliminates the verification of reports on paper, buying the paper, compiling the reports and organizing, and then mailing them.

Record-keeping service providers often resist changing the way they do things. This is especially true in the area of customer service, as they often feel their clients will not accept changes such as:

- Sending paper statements less frequently
- Leveraging the Internet for transactions and inquiry
- Plan-sponsor reports on the Internet

Back in the days when interactive voice response first became prevalent, clients would say that they didn't want to adopt the new technology, because it would take away from the employees' work time. In reality, it reduced their anxiety and actually resulted in higher quality information in less time. The same is occurring with the Internet, as the Internet can provide virtually every document associated with the plan. It is good to want to provide the highest level of service, but make sure it is what your end-users will want, and not what you currently perceive as the highest level of service.

Work with Your Clients and Make Them Part of the Process

Ultimately, the best way to leverage your clients is to work with them and make them a part of the process.

- **Set-up a quarterly or semi-annual meeting with your clients — even if by phone.** Spend 5 minutes to 1 hour discussing the process, any improvements, and proactively managing the next quarter's deliverables, such as any required compliance reports (especially if you need special input). Although the actual end-client is the participant, the plan sponsor needs to feel comfortable about the process.

- **Once again, make sure you drop clients that are unprofitable.** Inform them you are not making money and they will be better off with another firm. If they are nearby, do this in person, but if they require significant travel, set up a conference call, in advance. Make sure to include the investment advisor or consultant, if they are involved. You can send this message in a positive way by giving them the choice of increased fees, and offering the best alternatives.

- **Send an annual quality survey to all clients, investment advisors, and 1% of participants.** If you want inexpensive feedback, that is 100% unbiased, this is it.

The Expense Side: People and Process

Leveraging Your Partners and Vendors

From a record-keeper's perspective, I can't tell you how many times I have seen a strategic partner, such as a directed trustee, aggressively bid on new business with a competitor, when they should be focused on their current clients. Therefore, it is essential that you bid all outsourced services every 18 months.

Do not let your partners in delivering services become complacent, as they may be taking you for granted. Specifically, they may be giving more time, greater technology, and lower prices to new clients. This includes directed trustees/ trading partners, participant-communication partners, record-keeping technology, etc. Don't be bashful about running a business. Be professional in the process, as this process is better than threatening your book of business. By bidding out the services, you will also stay in tune with the latest trends. Bidding out does not mean a guaranteed change, and the change should not be based solely on price, as you will pay a price for changing a significant partner.

The investment industry needs you more than you need them. Brokers and advisors simply want to sell 401(k) plans. That's the good news for the record keepers, as this can eliminate the need for hiring a sales staff. However, if the relationships are not solid, the brokers and advisors may go elsewhere. In addition, it is incumbent upon the advisor to be able to sell their strategic advantage, which is generally their expertise (or often simply selling themselves). A majority of advisors/brokers focus on out-of-pocket price, hence more pressure on the record keepers. Therefore, partner with the brokers and investment advisors you are comfortable with and make it a long-term relationship.

Mutual-fund companies simply want their funds in the plans, so they target the directed trustee, record keepers, and platforms. You must ensure you are receiving the highest level of revenue sharing within their investment expense, as compared to their partners.

The Major Expenses of Running a Practice

A record-keeping service provider is only as strong as its people and the process running its record-keeping software system. In the pre-Internet age, record keepers were only as good as their record-keeping system and people. Today, it is a combination of their website technology and its integration with the basic record-keeping technology. As discussed earlier, technology to the end consumer may seem inexpensive; however, it certainly is not for the firms using technology to deliver the end product. With Congress continuing to alter ERISA, it is virtually impossible for a record-keeping service provider to develop its own technology, let alone maintain a system. Hence, record-keeping service providers must continue to pressure their software providers for quality issues and new releases. Unfortunately with the low numbers of competent record-keeping software providers, the record-keeping service providers' leverage is decreasing. Record-keeping service providers have the following options related to record-keeping administration software:

- Buy the code and maintain it themselves.
- Buy the system and pay for maintenance.
- Lease (lower upfront costs, but generally a higher long-term fee, as the fee may be participant-based).

The next generation of service to the record-keeping service provider will introduce an ASP (Application Service Provider) model that reduces software and hardware fees. Other key benefits from the ASP model include:

- The service or application can be securely run from any computer, anywhere, at any time.
- The ASP will be responsible for upkeep of the service provided, rather than an internal IT department. Therefore, money is saved on hardware, support, maintenance, upgrades and deployment without forfeiting functionality and business return.
- The Service Level Agreement (SLA) you have with the ASP guarantees you dedicated technical support. This means you are guaranteed disaster recovery, better application availability, better data security, more frequent data backups, and basic, centralized technical support.

In short, ASPs enable companies to focus their resources on what they do best, rather than upon information technology.

When analyzing the costs for running a record-keeping administration service firm, the costs, in order of percentage, are:

- People
- Record-keeping software
- Hardware/software technology (to support all services)
- Office space
- Training
- Inefficiency of Operations (As discussed above this may be the most important component, as the managers and teams make these decisions. The cost of a poor decision will have an effect for many years to come, and, in fact, could irreparably harm the firm. The managers

have the key to success, which is to drive costs down to appropriate levels, while ensuring high quality.) Key area's to focus on:

– Redundancy of tasks
– Too many layers of client contacts
– Sacred Cows (think change)
– Too many meetings
– Lack of empowerment at all levels
– Lack of training
– No documentation of the process

Breaking this down into its components, there are three key areas:

1. **People** — It is crucial to have compensation, staffing and training plans in place. Selection of managers and key decision makers is just as important. If you are not thinking offshore (overseas), your competitors are.

2. **Technology** — You must think long term, and leverage legacy systems with new technology. This business is evolving to one of system integration. The firms that best integrate the following systems will win:

– Recordkeeping administration
– Day to Day recordkeeping
– Compliance
– Directed Trustee/Clearing
– Brokerage Accounts
– Health & Welfare systems
– Defined Benefit systems (on demand projections)
– Payroll
– HR Systems

If you have a legacy system, you may be at the mercy of the software provider for change, which means you are highly dependent on their success for your success.

3. **Proof and Controls/Operation Efficiency** — Are you providing services as efficiently and effectively as possible?

The Most Important Resource — People

Without a doubt, the most important element to success is the people involved. Hiring good people that serve your clients' needs allows your record-keeping business to grow and become more profitable. Conversely, keeping people that are overpaid or who negatively influence the client or teams, impacts the bottom line negatively. While common sense dictates you should deal with the employees who are not a good fit, your initial reaction may be that trained resources are difficult to replace. A senior person who can get a lot of work done, compared to others, but has issues dealing with negativity, may be the hardest to address. Ask yourself, and your managers, the following questions:

- Will your team benefit more in the long term if this person is no longer around?
- Will your clients benefit, long term, if this person is no longer around?
- Will you lose other good people because this person is around?
- If the person is that good, is there anything they can do that does not showcase their weakness, or affect the team?

The opposite problem is that many record-keeping professionals think the grass is greener at other firms. Though this may be true in select cases, the day-to-day issues of record keeping are the same anywhere you go.

Why do record-keeping professionals leave?

1. Higher pay (Another firm is always desperate for an experienced person.)

2. Seeking a better environment

- Honest environment (about hours, pay, etc.)
- Positive energy
- Manager support

3. Leave the Business (eating nails for breakfast is not for me)

This is a high-turnover business, as not everyone enjoys the inherent pressures. In the 1980s, there was no formal training process, nor any accredited processes. Today, there are several excellent options for continued training: NIPA, ASPA, SPARK, and CEBS. However, very few companies incorporate additional educational benefits to their employees for these advanced degrees in their compensation packages.

What makes this situation more difficult is that in the mid-1990s, when the industry exploded, firms had to overpay for talent, at all levels. In recent years, all levels have seen a more defined approach to compensation, and many managers have experienced lay-offs or lower salaries. The days of moving from one service provider to the next, to increase compensation, are over. From the firms' point of view, it is better to train and keep current employees, as opposed to hiring from the outside, where you face the risk of upsetting the team chemistry, especially if your valued senior members are set in their ways.

Additionally, it really takes at least one year for a person to get acclimated to the process, and upwards of three years before a person can understand the process, the law, and the technology completely. Therefore, it is incumbent upon us to keep the employees that we have trained. It is important to note that this process starts in the hiring phase. As in every business, if you take the "warm-body" approach, you will lose. It is crucial to take the time up front to hire the right people.

If you keep your good employees long term, your turnover and training costs will be lower, and most importantly, your operational efficiency will be as close to maximum as possible! It all starts with creating a compensation plan and hiring strategy (see next sub-topic).

Promoting from within, and retaining senior managers, continues to build on the successful foundation. Your senior management team will make virtually every important strategy and process flow decision, so it is crucial to have experienced managers that have a passion for the company and its clients.

The Staffing Plan

Hire in advance by using the "Funnel Sales-Tracking Process," which is a method that uses regression-analysis tools to predict new business levels 3-6 months in advance. Advance knowledge of anticipated increases in business volume allows record-keeping service providers to hire and properly train employees as needed, rather than scrambling to fill an unexpected void. The benefits are fourfold:

1. Can train appropriately
2. Coverage for busy days or when people are out
3. Do not have to panic when someone leaves the firm
4. Shows commitment to the team that are you thinking ahead and are really focused on customer service, not just the bottom line

Initially, one would think this is more expensive; however, over time it is actually less expensive. If you are forced to hire when needed, especially after an employee has just left, it may cause you to make a decision to hire inappropriately, including:

- Hiring someone who is above your budget or compensation range
- Hiring someone who does not fit with the team
- Hiring two people at entry levels, in the hopes that two inexperienced people can make up for the experienced person leaving
- Being forced to use an expensive recruiting service

Promote from within when at all possible. It is worth the risk, as it strongly encourages others to achieve their goals and creates a better working environment. Promoting from the outside can lead to the following issues:

- The new-hire is an unknown entity.
- Current staff feels employer has no confidence in them.
- New managers like to do things their own way and like to bring in their own people (both may be counter to the culture you are trying to build).

There is a right time and place for hiring from the outside, but it is important, when you do this, that the team understands why. Include them in the hiring process. Blindsiding the team not only makes them uncomfortable, but also makes things more difficult for the new manager.

Student Interns

Ultimately, you should be continually interviewing by leveraging the local universities, especially through a part-time program for students. The intern, or part-time process, is an excellent way to find future full-time candidates and to staff day-to-day tasks, such as filing and downloading files in a cost-effective manner. The intern's, or part-time employee's, compensation is much less than that of full-time employees (and does not include benefits), but is deemed a high wage by the college students. Furthermore, part-timers can greatly help during the busy period in the first three months of a calendar year. As a side note, a great way to find out if a person has management potential is to start management candidates out by managing the part-time employees and interns. They will find it especially challenging to manage work schedules and to ensure that the day-to-day tasks assigned to the part-timers are accomplished (especially with the last-second no-shows on a Friday night).

The Selection Process

Make the interview process a habit — well defined and repeatable. Developing and implementing such a process, and ensuring it is used *each and every time* you bring someone into your organization, streamlines the process for everyone involved. It also ensures your hiring processes are consistent. It is important to avoid even the appearance of inconsistent or discriminatory hiring processes, even inadvertently.

When developing a selection process, keep the following steps in mind:

- Develop job-related criteria for each job category in your firm (ensuring that each criterion is measurable, and document the measurement for each).
- Define which criteria are must-haves (criteria that must exist in order to consider a candidate for a particular position, e.g. college degree)
- Prioritize each remaining criterion in comparison to the others, using a consistent weighting scale.
- Weigh the importance of deviation from each remaining criterion (e.g. how important is it if a particular candidate does not meet a particular criterion).
- Ensure all team members participating in hiring understand the criteria, and their weights. Periodically review the criteria to refresh the team's understanding.
- When hiring for a new position, ensure that all candidates are evaluated using the same pre-determined criteria.
- Prescreen candidates, using the "must-haves."
- Rank candidates based on how well they meet the pre-defined criteria.
- Rank candidates based on how much they deviate from any particular criteria.
- Compare the above rankings and eliminate candidates who do not rise to the top of both rankings.
- When making a final selection, document the ranking of the selected person, and the reasons why they were chosen (e.g. #1 ranked across all categories).

A good practice is to keep a record of the data from each ranking process. Not only is this a valuable record if there are any hiring disputes, but also the data can be periodically compared against performance, and the hiring criteria adjusted accordingly.

Compensation

It is very important to establish guidelines, up front, with all candidates in terms of salary and expectations. Too many record-keeping service providers negotiate these expectations with entry-level candidates. Of course, this creates dissent immediately among other team members. Therefore, it is best to define the compensation packages before beginning the interviewing process for entry-level candidates. These compensation packages should be based on the following:

- Base salary
- Bonus based on profitability and quality scores
- Increase in salary immediately upon successfully completing an accredited program such as ASPA (no exceptions)
- A second increase in base salary upon completion of your internal training program (my recommendation is target this for the 18-month review)

It is also important to create grade classes within job categories, to eliminate discrepancies among teammates, or for those cases when you must hire from the outside. Create grade classes detailing the skills necessary to achieve the class. For example, create 3-4 levels for record-keeping administrators and managers.

Do not deviate from the pay grades to hire from the outside. If you do, be prepared for problems in the long term, especially from the people that have been with you for a long time.

It is crucial that all employees take part in the profitability and the quality of the firm. Because of this, it is an excellent idea to incorporate a profit-sharing component in the retirement plan, or a bonus structure. It is important, however, to set up a plan that is achievable, as the last thing you want to do is implement a plan that does not reap any actual rewards.

A final note on compensation: The DOL has instructed certain record-keeping service providers that entry-level administrators must be paid overtime. In the case I was involved with, the young DOL reviewer (who was anti-business) determined that the entry-level administrator was not making day-to-day decisions. I'll bet most of the record keepers out there would disagree with that, after having to pay up for their judgement errors. The result of the DOL decision is some record-keeping service providers are forced to change their bene-fit plans, away from flex time and bonus-based pay.

Training

Make training a priority, and budget the hard dollars and employees' time. The better the training, the more efficient the process — and the better the prod-uct and service. Do not make the mistake most firms make, which is to have employees learn while doing the job. Bring in experts from the outside to train employees. Encourage managers to receive their MBAs. The management staff at many record-keeping service providers is excellent at record keeping and consulting, but has little or no formal training in management. This does not mean that all managers need an MBA, but specific management training should be identified and completed at each level.

The best firms have catalogues of training with dates scheduled throughout the coming year. They include internal and external programs. In fact, I encourage record-keeping service providers to have entry-level employees learn the process for the first 1-3 months, with no specific work assignments.

The Operations Decision — Proof and controls

With the increase in on-demand service levels, record keepers have also faced a downturn in what used to be the pressure-packed delivery of participant statements. As a record keeper in the pre-Internet era, if you delivered the wrong data, you were essentially dead in the water in the future. Quarter-ends were miserable, with the added proof and controls and the pressure to print the statements with cool color graphics. Of course the latter was a real pain, as you had to have special paper and the alignment always had to be correct. If you outsourced it, you had a good chance the printer didn't check the alignment, or actual printing, as closely as you would. Some of the all-time worst errors:

- Printing statements on two pages with no page breaks, so every employee got to see a portion of someone else's record along with their own
- Printing the statements on the wrong custom paper, which meant the participants received accurate statements, but the logo of the company was not theirs
- Printing from the wrong file, so everything was wrong
- Not printing a certain investment fund; hence, statement did not add up

To this day, when participants receive statements, the toughest issue you have to face is that of the reported earnings by the mutual funds as compared to their actual earnings on their statements. **If you had to perform just one proof and control, this is the proof and control you should employ.** Any discrepancies over 10 basis points must be explained. The best statements to check are the ones with no activity, as they should be within 1 basis point every time. Why are there differences?

- Timing of inflow or outflow
- Transfers by the participant
- Fees deducted at the participant level (record-keeping or investment advisory fees)
- An error by the record keeper

When checking a statement with no activity, there are only two reasons there are a difference — either a record-keeping error, or fees were deducted from the account. Daily valuation has reduced the number of errors, however in a volatile market, even missing a day can have a major impact on the performance.

This is why I have stated that the most important task a record keeper performs is ensuring timely contributions and distributions. **Don't ever make a decision not to invest because you are busy, as even one day can be very costly.**

From a management perspective, errors in human judgment can be the most costly. It is a judgment call as to:

- when you have too many proof and controls in place, and
- when you do not have enough proof and controls (leading to reruns and errors, which lead to write-offs to make the accounts whole).

The irony is that an outsider's first response to an error is, "How could you make such a stupid mistake? Why don't you have a proof and control in place?" Thus, a good policy for your teams is to demand that they **always** follow **all** proof and controls, as this will eliminate virtually all issues. Furthermore, you should make it clear to your teams that if even one is bypassed, it could lead to immediate termination. This will be difficult to enforce, especially if you are understaffed or under trained; however, it will set the tone.

Where do you draw the line on proof and controls? Well, this, of course, depends on the type of business you serve. If you are using a black-box approach where all plans fit the same model, then it is easier to have the same proof and controls for all plans, which leads to lower training costs and less management overview. If your business is on the other extreme, whereby you allow maximum flexibility in plan design and investment selection, you may have to instill custom proof and controls. This leads to higher training costs, more management involvement, and a more defined team approach. The more defined team approach means you cannot put an employee onto a new team and expect them to hit the ground running.

As in many other areas of business, the key here is optimization. Balance the amount and type of controls against the value they bring, or the amount of risk they mitigate. When defining necessary proof and controls for a particular area of your business, keep in mind the following steps:

1. Determine the amount of risk, or variance, a particular area or project can tolerate
2. Identify areas of exposure
3. Define proof and controls which alleviate risk in exposed areas
4. Estimate both the cost of implementing/maintaining the proof or control and the value in elimination of risk
5. Compare the cost against the value and implement only those controls that have a positive ROI (return on investment).
6. Monitor the proof and controls in actual practice and make adjustments as necessary

The best process you can have in place is to meet with your operations team and encourage all parties to review all "sacred cows." These are processes that have been in place for years, which no one can explain why they are performed that way, other than it has been done that way for years. Compensate employees for bringing these up and presenting a solution. Let go of those managers who are holding onto sacred cows.

Defining the Processes

To functionalize or not to functionalize? This debate has been ongoing for the last ten years. Put simply, this means that one person works on a certain segment of the plan process for multiple plans, but does not complete the entire process for any plan. The trends lately are to a modified functionalized environment, with services in the following functional areas:

- Customer Service Reps (for incoming phone calls and Internet access)
- Compliance Services (Form 5500s and all required testing)
- Account Management
- Daily Processing—Proof and controls
- Downloading Prices

Essentially, you have three choices:

1. Functionalize
2. One person, per client, for everything
3. Combination of both

The one person approach represents issues when they are out, or leave the firm. Thinking ahead, the one person performing all functions approach has merits for those employees working at home. Functionalizing often makes it difficult for each person to understand the whole process; they may be at a short-term disadvantage for management positions. However, this can be resolved through a commitment to cross-train in all areas and to transition employees to all functions in their first two years.

Manage to Your Goals

The red flags I see when visiting Operation Groups are:

- Lack of accountability at all levels
- No quality measurements
- Lack of managing to deadlines or setting deadlines

You cannot meet market or client expectations, let alone promised service goals if you are not tracking them. If an operations manager provides an excuse or a reason not to set deadlines or quality standards, then most likely you have a personnel issue. The senior managers set the tone not only for service expectations for the client, but the culture within the company. We are in a service industry that requires providing dates of delivery for day-to-day tasks and major service or software releases. If you do not provide them, why should any work with you?

Setting the right goals and measurements are just as important as the measuring process itself. Simply stated, I have seen many firms fall under the category of "Laws of Unintended Consequences." Although it is better to set and measure to goals, then not to, by setting the wrong standards can result in decrease service levels. This is because employees know how they will be evaluated and paid. Therefore when setting your goals, think of the following:

- Your clients—What is most important to them?
- Set goals at the company, team, and individual level. Make sure they complement each other.
- Encourage employees to improve the process

One area of the "Law of Unintended Consequences" that I see happen frequently in this business is when companies focus on cost reduction by encouraging Call Center representative to get off the phone quickly or resolve the problem by turning it back to the client or partner. The obvious result may include reduced costs, however it often results in increased costs as the net results are:

- Reduced Customer Service
- More Phone Calls
- Increased escalations to higher paid employees
- Lost Business

You Have Read This Chapter and Determined You Need to Change

Many companies know they need to change, but try it in a manner that is doomed for failure. Why?

- Employees are tired of the Management Theory of the Month or Week Club
- Employees are not ready to change
- Employees do not understand the need to change
- Senior management or key agents of change do not follow through with passion and conviction

There are plenty of books and articles as to best practices for the change process. I encourage all senior managers to read these books and articles often, as they stress change can only happen if diagnosed correctly. Most companies will need to bring in an expert from the outside to achieve results, as the experts will be able to push back at senior manager levels to affect change. In some cases (most), the root cause is the senior manager, which can only be fixed by changing their ways or eliminating them. If you are embarking on a change process, it is important to understand the three phases:

1. **Diagnosis Phase** — Identify the symptoms and find the root cause.
2. **Change Readiness** — Employees and managers must be ready for change. Some of the best ways to achieve this are to:
   - Include the employees in the change process
   - Show them how the competitors are better
   - Use outside influencers, such as consultants or the industry press.
   - Select change agents that are influencers and passionate about the company and industry.
   - Clearly articulate the reasons for the change and the end results of the change process
3. **Implementation Phase** — It is important to not only implement the changes, but measure the progress of the change in terms of quality, process efficiency, employee satisfaction, and firm financials.

It is important to include the entire company in the change process. By being upfront and honest with employees, vendors, partners, and clients will buy you the goodwill you will need to enact change.

In Review

Create a business plan and marketing strategy and review it every quarter in macro and in detail every 18 months. The most difficult part of my job as a business consultant is talking about the negative aspects, which is crucial to creating a successful business plan. It is important to discuss and review the following:

- **Disaster recovery** — Discuss what to do if your offices are out of commission for any time. (Don't let the 'it can't happen to me' approach pass, as it happens to many good businesses.)
- **Loss of key people** — Perform 'what if' scenarios and determine a course of action in advance.

- **Loss of business** — Perform 'what if' scenarios, especially if over 10% of your revenue is with one client, or is tied to a certain partner or advisor.
- **Annual staff reviews** — Create an annual review process for your staff that is substantive and fair. (Try to incorporate as much objective evidence as possible, such as the ability to perform certain tasks, quality scores, etc. The subjective ranking should represent less than 50% of the review. It is crucial that annual reviews are performed on time and reviewed by all managers. Some firms employ a forced ranking process, to ensure the top employees receive the best pay increases, and the very bottom employees are given every chance to succeed . . . or, as was done at GE, to eliminate them if they are on the list twice in a row).
- **Marketing strategy** — Discuss the marketplace and your value proposition.

CHAPTER XI

Value of a Record-Keeping Practice

The days of selling a record-keeping practice at five times a multiple of revenues are long gone. In fact, there are several firms targeting record-keeping service providers as a means to grow quickly, but the price they are paying is often limited to a 'share-only deal' or, at maximum, a multiple of profits. If cash is involved in the transaction, it is generally limited to a multiple of profits on an earn-out basis.

Record-keeping service providers have another significant value in addition to their administration clients, and that is their relationship with the client. It is crucial to recognize the needs of your clients, and the key administrative functions necessary for your clients, including, not only, defined-contribution administration, but also the following areas:

- Defined-contribution plan design and compliance
- Payroll services
- Health & welfare plan design
- Claims processing
- Cobra administration
- Retirement planning
- Accounting services

As a participant in any company or plan, your clients typically want one service: *on-demand access to all employee benefits information, complete with the ability to ask questions and receive answers in a timely manner.*

As a plan sponsor or company, your goal should be to increase the value of the employee benefits, as it is a significant portion of an employee's overall compensation. Your role is to deliver the message in a medium that is fast, easy to use, and substantive (perhaps a website for inquiry and transaction purposes).

As a record-keeping service provider, record-keeping administration is only one piece of the employee-benefit puzzle, which for the last 10-12 years, has been a stand-alone sale. This will not be the case in the future, as companies will want one site for all benefits.

From a record-keeping-only perspective, your risks are high, as the current focus is:

- Ease of participant use (IVR and Internet)
- Compliance services to the plan sponsor
- Fees/flexibility

Savvy firms will be able to aggressively price the entire employee-benefits package, or enter into new partnerships to better achieve the goals of the participant and plan sponsor.

Partnerships, Acquisitions and Mergers

Every day is the right time to leverage your practice for a merger, key partnership, or outright sale. Complete the following items to determine how much control you have of your business, which translates into a higher valuation (price):

1. Total revenues of business you won directly, or now control directly (business wins through investment advisors, brokers, and strategic partners do not count)
2. Recurring revenue, as a percentage of annual income
3. Percentage of clients you can introduce to new lines of business
4. List your top five clients, and indicate the percentage of overall revenue (addresses risk)

Several aggregators will simply look to acquire firms that have a good book of business, but are inefficient or do not leverage the investment industry. Some firms can be acquired, and essentially paid for, by simply switching the directed-trustee solution, which can better leverage revenue-sharing and preferred-marketing relationships with certain fund families.

Know your expertise, and your customer service approach. Regardless if you are a low-cost or a premium-service provider, identify areas of expertise, such as:

- Cutting-edge technology
- Participant communications
- Strong distribution channel

No one firm is great at every component, so be honest with your review. Of the thousands of record keepers, all of them use a total of 5-6 different record-keeping systems. In other words, the competitive advantage is not the record keeping system, unless there is a paradigm shift, in the future, that allows one record-keeping system to significantly differentiate itself in service. Therefore, for record-keeping service providers to distinguish themselves, their process, packaging and people will make the difference. Reputation is subjective, but the following statistics will back it up:

- Customer satisfaction surveys
- Consistent new business numbers
- Low client turnover
- Low internal turnover (a certain amount is expected in the first two years)

The better prepared you are on all of the above, the higher the value of your company.

Don't be afraid to explore partnerships or entertain offers from other firms. However, do not show your financials unless you are serious, as no matter how many non-disclosure agreements are signed, word leaks. Also, if you are talking to other firms, make sure you understand their acquisition strategy, as some firms look to buy value, and others look for quality or to expand into a new line of business. You certainly do not want to have the marketplace discussing the fact that you may be selling your firm, especially for the wrong reasons, as this may scare away new business.

Your marketing strategy can increase the value of your firm, simply through branding. Also, your partnerships and vendors are an indication of who you do business with, and how you do it, and is often used as due diligence in partnership, merger, or acquisition talks. Hence, leverage your practice and treat all parties as you would like to be treated, and this will certainly increase the value of your firm. As an example, ask the directed trustees what the best firms are in the business. They can tell you, based on the turnover stats, their relationship, and their discussions with the clients directly.

The winning strategy is simply taking the time to perform honest internal reviews, having a smart marketing strategy, and a good business plan. If you are going down the path of merging or selling your practice, perform your due diligence on the new firm, as they will be your new partner or boss. Find out early what type of offer they are considering based on general discussions, and if they ask what it is going to take for you to sell, be prepared to give them a direct and specific answer.

If your firm is in an acquisition mode, make sure you perform you initial analysis from the following information:

1. A list at the client level that includes the following information:
   - Client Name (this can be blacked out or replaced with a number)
   - Recurring Fee
   - Number of Participants
   - Type of Plan (401(k), PS, MP, 457, 403(b), etc)
   - Assets by Fund (with ticker)
   - Client Hire Date (approximate, for example Q1 1998)
   - Control of Client
     - Direct (D)
     - By Broker (B)
     - By Investment Advisor (F for fee for Service)

2. Audited Financial Statements that that break down the revenues in the following categories:
   - Recurring Recordkeeping/Administration Revenue (includes revenue sharing)
   - One-Time Consulting Revenue (the last two years may have higher numbers because of required doc changes). The three sub categories are consulting fees, conversion fees, and termination fees
   - Indirects — Marketing Fees or soft dollar fees

3. A copy of the last two SAS70's

4. Copies of all vendor contracts with directed trustees, communication firms, printing shops, technology firms, etc.

5. A copy of three recent RFP's sent to defined contribution prospects.

6. Copies of all agreements with fund groups relating to Sub-Transfer Agent (or any related contracts related to direct revenue sharing).

7. Copies of your standard client service agreements (with the plan sponsor). If it has changed in the last three years, include the current and prior agreements.

Customer Satisfaction Surveys — Know Your Value

In this industry, as in any other, the only way to truly know what end users think of your services is to ask them. Whether you are a broker or record-keeping service provider, you should hire a firm to perform a customer quality survey at least once every other year. Excellent results are great marketing tools and increase the value of your firm or practice. Poor results tell you where to focus. When implementing a survey process, hire an outside firm with a reputation for achieving accurate, unbiased results. Make sure all areas of service are measured, including the areas you know are weak.

From a management perspective, if you are tying the results to compensation or bonus, set realistic, but high, goals for satisfaction. Make sure that everyone is being measured and communicate your expectations of just what outstanding service means.

In addition to formal customer surveys, make sure your senior managers are calling or visiting the clients and asking for feedback. Ask the tough questions, and document the answers for all. Make sure you randomly monitor customer-service calls or chats, and ensure that both your customer and your service personnel know this may be happening. Not only will it help to make sure your team is performing at its best, but it will allow you to hear the kinds of issues end-users are having. Very few firms perform this function, which translates to decision makers making uninformed decisions related to service. The best firms and managers proactively manage by details.

CHAPTER XII

How to Be Successful in the Retirement Industry

Finding the Right Job

Almost anyone can be successful in this industry, as there are so many different types of jobs. Here are some of the job classifications, with brief descriptions and some of the traits needed for success:

- **Record-Keeping Administration** (record-keeping service providers and directed trustees) — Love computers, numbers, and people
- **Compliance** (attorneys and consultants) — Enjoy reading regulations and designing plans, finding solutions or completing government forms and completing required tests
- **Accounting/Audit** — Plans (greater than 100 participants) need to be audited and the service providers need true SAS70 audits
- **Account Managers** — Serving the client, working with people and managing client expectations, as well as working with internal operations team; good people skills
- **Communications** — Includes companies that focus on participant communications, creation of prototype plan documents and SPDs, as well as creation of all required forms. Strong writing skills are needed.
- **Managers** — Of record keeping, directed trustees, etc.
- **Technology/Software** — Designers, programmers, etc.
- **Investment Management** — Investment advisors, brokers, and managers of money
- **Human Resources at the Client** — Enjoy working with people and vendors (the latter is very difficult)
- **Salespeople**

The best salespersons, account managers, and consultants in this business are the ones that know the business, either by starting out as a record keeper, or administrator, or by dedicating their careers to the business. As a record-keeping administrator, you get to see everything work (or not work) and most likely have seen many errors over the course of 3-5 years — not only in process, but also in plan design, investment management, and compliance. The difference between the experts and the rest of the pack is simple: the experts can explain the process down to the finite steps, and can perform all compliance testing on paper (or at least explain how). That doesn't mean you can't learn the business by reading, accreditation, or taking the time to learn from professionals; it just requires more effort and dedication.

Starting out in this industry

Every city has record-keeping service providers and investment firms that are hiring at entry level. Before sending your resume to all of these providers, take 2-3 weeks to study the industry through journals, websites, and interviews with people who work in the industry. In your cover letter, discuss why you would make a good record keeper or customer service representative, by equating school or work experience into the process. Remember these key characteristics:

- You enjoy working with computers and have relevant experience in this area.
- You are comfortable with math and, again, provide reasons/experience.
- You enjoy serving the customer, at the participant level, and, of course, can provide experience.

Anyone can claim they are a hard worker and are willing to put in long hours (which is pretty standard), but very few take the time to understand the industry. In fact, completing the two take-home courses from ASPA will make it hard for a record-keeping service provider to deny an interview, as you went out of your way to learn the industry, have completed the courses, and are still interested in the business.

Most record keepers are perpetually hiring, so if you really want a job in this industry you can most likely find one.

Moving to a new firm

Remember, the grass is not always greener on the other side of the fence. Write down your priorities for the perfect job, and don't just interview with one firm or accept the first job offered. Turn the process into a mutual interview and get to know the service provider's processes. Do they meet your expectations? Is it the type of environment you would be comfortable in? Make sure you interview with your eventual boss and at least 2-3 of the people you will be working with. In this industry, people love to talk, so you should be able to get the inside scoop easily.

This is important for you, as a bad move can affect not only your professional career but also your personal life. It is also important for you to get a contract you are comfortable with. Don't just sign anything; make sure the terms are what you discussed, including the confidentiality and no-compete clauses. If there is a bonus involved, get the facts and don't just agree verbally. Ask how long they have had the bonus program, how many years they have allocated a bonus, and who received it.

Having said this, many record-keeping service providers do not have a strong interview process, as outlined earlier. This will be a tip-off as to their level of organization. Many firms simply try to hire a good person who is knowledgeable about the business.

This business is not for everyone, but there is a good fit for almost anyone in this sector. If you have three years of record-keeping administration and want to transition to a different position, start those discussions with your current employer. If you work for a small firm, this may be more difficult, so you may have to look elsewhere for a specialized position in participant communications, account management, or sales. The best way to find your best-fit job is to take part in your local and regional organizations. Many of these organizations meet frequently, and informally, and are often your best way to find out about great opportunities.

Getting Ahead in This Business

If you can remember these three mantras, it will be hard for you not to reap your just rewards in this industry:

1. Strive to make everyone around you look good
2. Place the client first, team second, and yourself third
3. Proactively manage your clients, team/boss, and vendors (e-mails and phone calls on a consistent basis)

Being the best you can be

You cannot be the best record-keeping administrator overnight, as it takes at least three years to understand and learn all the nuances. This does not preclude you from being the best you can be each day for your client and team. Strive to:

- Be organized, especially your calendar and client folders.
- Complete tasks on time (and accurately).
- Proactively manage your clients and managers (the latter should be each day).

Complaining about your manager (whether justly or not), the company, or your clients does not help anyone. Positive energy breeds positive energy, and negative energy breeds the same. Very rarely does a negative-energy person advance in this business, or any other. Constructive criticism of a process, accompanied with suggestions or options to change, is not negative energy. Simply saying a process 'stinks' is negative energy.

Maintain positive energy, serve your clients well (including your internal clients), and make everyone around you look good. Then simply read about the business every day on the Internet, and find people who display a real passion for this industry. These are the people to enjoy lunch, coffee or breaks with. Their insight will be invaluable.

What to Avoid at All Costs

Now for the Don'ts:
1. Don't blame others for your inability to complete your projects or work.
2. Don't fail to notify the appropriate parties if your work cannot be completed on time (and be sure to say why).
3. Don't send negative e-mails about people in the workplace, as the first course of action. These can be easily misinterpreted. A better of way of handling this is by phone, first, or in person.

4. Don't ever compare your workload with others in discussions with managers, peers, etc. Every client is different, so it is difficult to actually compare workloads. Especially don't make this error in formal reviews.

5. Don't ever say anything negative to a client. Not only does this not help you, it hurts your company. No matter how close you are to your client, including their sensitivities to your situation, it will get passed on to their teammates and eventually all decision-makers of both firms.

6. Do not tell your teammates and peers that you are unhappy and are looking. Keep this to yourself.

7. Don't stay on a job you are uncomfortable with or don't like. Be honest with everyone, and you will generate a lot of people who will help you find a job internally or externally.

8. Don't ever leave a client, vendor, or teammate in doubt about when the deliverables are due. Surprisingly, I hear people say they don't want to promise a date, because they don't know if they can meet it, and it is better to not give a date. In order to teach these folks about customer service, I ask them what they would think if their dry cleaner didn't provide a turnaround time, or the next time they asked for a cab, no arrival time was provided.. Every client deserves a schedule.

9. If there is a hot issue related to deliverables, or, potentially, an error, don't avoid the client. The last thing you should do is avoid the client. The right way is to hit the issue head on, and be honest.

It is not that hard to make a good living in this business and have fun. Find a company with an excellent environment that has a job that fits your needs.

Closing

The winning firms will have the following characteristics

- A sound Business Strategy that is reviewed at minimum annually
- Thinks out of the box (such as considering offshore capabilities or new business lines)
- Listens to the client and continues to solve their 'distress' issues
- Are system integrators
- Operation Efficient

- Think long term (such as one retirement account for defined contribution plans, ERSA's, and privatized social security)

The best firms welcome change in our industry, not fear it, as these are new opportunities to prove to their clients they are the firm to work with. Firms that fear change or are in self-preservation mode are easy to spot. Clients want to work with firms that can change and want to have long term relationships.

This business is a lot of fun and will be around for a long time. The best firms encourage change in our industry, not fear it. Think opportunity in times of change, not self preservation. For those of us who have been around for a long time, it is up to us to make sure we keep it fun. Most importantly, we need to make sure all professionals are acting ethically. Every one of us in the industry — service or client side — should be encouraging full disclosure of fees and revenues.

Service-provider contracts should be direct and to the point. Let's reduce the amount of indemnification clauses and increase the amount of responsibility. If a service provider is going to limit their liability to a certain dollar amount, or not take responsibility for a function they are performing, put it in **bold** in the contract. The contract should reflect the sales process.

Do the right thing at all times. It is an honor to be serving in this profession with dedicated and honest people. The employee-benefits industry is one of high standards and high ethics; let's keep it that way.

Glossary of Terms

401(k) Plan
A defined-contribution plan that permits employees to deduct a portion of their salary from their paycheck and contribute to an account before taxation. Employers may also make contributions to a participant's account, called a company match. Federal (and sometimes state) taxes on contributions and investment earnings are "deferred" (i.e. postponed) until the participant takes money out of the plan in a distribution (typically at retirement).

403(b) Plan
Also known as a *tax-sheltered annuity* (TSA), a 403(b) provides a tax shelter for 501(c)(3) tax-exempt employers (which include public schools). Employers qualifying for a 403(b) plan may defer taxes on contributions to certain annuity contracts or custodial accounts.

404(c) Plan
The ERISA Code for defined-contribution plan that passes a portion of the plan sponsor's fiduciary responsibility on to the participant, if the participant follows the approximate 21 guidelines explicitly.

Active Management
The style of a professional investment or mutual-fund manager who believes that they can add value from either stock picking or market timing.

Accrued Benefits
Retirement benefits earned to date by an employee, which will be expressed in a 401(k) plan in terms of the amount in the employee's account.

Actual Deferral Percentage (ADP)
An anti-discrimination test that compares the amount deferred by highly compensated employees to the deferrals of non-highly compensated employees.

Asset Allocation
An employee's division of money between different types of investment choices. An example of asset allocation would be 70 percent stocks and 30 percent bonds.

Alternate Payee
A person other than a plan participant (such as a spouse, former spouse, child, etc.) who, under a domestic relations order (see *qualified domestic relations order*), has a right to receive all or some of a participant's pension benefits.

Annual Audit
Federal law requires that an independent auditor audit all plans with more than 100 participants. It is also common to refer to a DOL or IRS examination of a plan as a plan audit.

Annual Report
A document filed annually (Form 5500) with the IRS that reports pension-plan information for a particular year, including such items as participation, funding, and administration.

Annuity
A contract providing retirement income at regular intervals. See also *qualified joint and survivor annuity*.

Automatic Deferral Default Percentage
The percentage of pay that is taken pre-tax and put into a plan when an employee is enrolled via an automatic enrollment feature. The typical automatic deferral default percentage is 3 percent of pay. Participants can generally choose to defer an amount other than the default percentage.

Automatic Enrollment
The practice of enrolling all eligible employees in a plan and beginning participant deferrals without requiring the employees to submit a request to participate. Plan design specifies how these automatic deferrals will be invested.

Employees who do not want to make contributions must actively file a request to be excluded from the plan. Participants can generally change the amount of pay that is deferred and how it is invested.

Balance Forward
This refers to all defined-contribution plans that are not updated daily, whereby participant accounts are updated monthly, quarterly, or annually. These plans should be referred to as traditional. ESOP plans and one-fund money-purchase plans are plans that are generally updated in a traditional environment.

Basis Points
A basis point is 1/100th of a percent (100 basis points equals one percent). Many trustees and record-keeping service providers charge fees based on assets in terms of basis points.

Beneficiary
A person, persons or trust designated to receive the plan benefits of a participant in the event of the participant's death.

Black Box
A service provider that does not provide custom services and will only accept business in their model. For example, a recordkeeper may choose only to serve plans that fit the following criteria:
- Use their prototype document
- Use their proprietary funds
- Payroll input must be in their format
- No customization on participant communications (such as no paper participant statements)

Blackout Period
Also called a lockdown, transitional period or quiet period. This refers to the time when plan participants cannot access their accounts. These periods can be caused by a number of events, including a change in plan recordkeepers, a change in plan trustees, a change to daily valuation from monthly valuation, or a company merger or acquisition.

Bundled Service Providers
See *Closed-architecture Service Providers*

Cafeteria Plan
In this plan employees may chose from a "menu" of two or more benefits.

Cash-Out
The distribution of assets from a plan to a participant prior to retirement, typically occurring when a participant has a balance under $5,000 and leaves a company without requesting to have their assets rolled over into an IRA or into a new employer's plan. Cash-outs are subject to federal withholding tax, and are subject to the ten percent early withdrawal, federal income-tax penalty if taken before age 59½.

Cash or Deferred Arrangement (CODA)
A type of profit-sharing or stock-bonus plan in which employees may defer current pre-tax compensation.

Cash or Deferred Election
A participant request to defer compensation, on a pre-tax basis, to a CODA Plan.

Cash Profit-sharing Plan
A type of profit-sharing plan in which the company makes contributions directly to employees in cash or stock. (This type of profit-sharing plan is not a qualified retirement plan.)

Cliff Vesting
A vesting schedule that gives an employee 100 percent ownership of company contributions after a specified number of years of service. For example, if you have a three-year cliff vesting schedule, all of the company contributions in your account in the first three years are still the company's. At three years, all monies in your company contribution account are 100% vested and yours.

Closed-architecture Service Providers
Previously referred to as bundled providers, these firms provide all services necessary for a defined-contribution plan.

Common Control
Businesses are under common control when one entity owns at least 80 percent of the stock, profit, or capital interest in the other organization, or when the same five or fewer people own a controlling interest in each entity.

Conversion
The process of changing from one service provider to another.

Custodian
A bank that holds a plan's assets.

Daily Valuation
The term used to describe how frequently a participant's account is updated. The most efficient and fastest way to update a participant's account is same day/late day; however, there are plans that are valued on a daily basis that are updated the next morning, with trades often pending over a one- to three-day period.

Deferred Profit-Sharing Plan
A type of qualified retirement plan in which the company makes contributions to individual participant accounts.

Deferral
A pre-tax contribution set aside from an employee's paycheck.

Defined-Benefit Plan
A retirement plan in which the sponsoring company provides a certain guaranteed benefit to participants based on a pre-determined formula.

Defined-Contribution Plan
An employer-sponsored plan in which contributions are made to individual participant accounts, and the final benefit consists solely of assets (including investment returns) that have accumulated in these individual accounts. Depending on the type of defined-contribution plan, contributions may be made either by the company, the participant, or both.

Department of Labor (DOL)
The U.S. Department of Labor (DOL) deals with issues related to the American workforce — including topics concerning pension and benefit plans. Through its branch agency, the Pension and Welfare Benefits Administration, the DOL is responsible for administering the provisions of Title I of ERISA, which regulates proper administration of plans.

Determination Letter
Document issued by the IRS formally recognizing that the plan meets the qualifications for tax-advantaged treatment.

Directed Trustee

Typically a bank or trust company that serves as a custodian of the plan's assets and performs all monetary transactions. Most directed trustees today are state chartered. Liability is limited to errors related to accurate and timely trades. The reason they are called 'directed trustees' is because they take all direction from the record-keeping service provider and are not responsible for any investment decisions on behalf of the plan or participant.

Disclosure

Plan sponsors must provide access to certain types of information for participants, including summary plan descriptions, summary of material modifications, and summary annual reports.

Discretionary Trustee

A bank or trust company that takes full fiduciary responsibility for the investments offered to the plan and how they are communicated to the participants.

Discrimination Testing

Tax qualified retirement plans must be administered in compliance with several regulations requiring numerical measurements. Typically, the process of determining whether the plan is in compliance is collectively called discrimination testing.

Distribution

Any payout made from a retirement plan. See also *lump-sum distribution* and *annuity*.

Early Withdrawal Penalty

There is a 10 percent early withdrawal, federal income-tax penalty for withdrawal of assets from a qualified retirement plan prior to age 59½. This 10 percent early withdrawal, federal income-tax penalty is in addition to regular federal and state tax (if applicable).

Eligibility

Conditions that must be met in order to participate in a plan, such as age or length of service requirements.

Eligible Employees

Employees who meet the requirements for participation in an employer-sponsored plan.

Employee Stock Ownership Plan (ESOP)

A qualified, defined-contribution plan in which plan assets are invested primarily, or exclusively, in the securities of the sponsoring employer.

ERISA

Plan sponsors are required by law to design and administer their plans in accordance with the Employee Retirement Income Security Act of 1974 (ERISA). Among its statutes, ERISA calls for proper plan reporting and disclosure to participants.

ERISA Rights Statement

ERISA requires that this document, explaining participant and beneficiary rights, be included within a summary plan description (SPD).

Excess Accumulations

The amount that a participant's required minimum distribution (after age 70½) surpasses the amount distributed. When distributions reach 50 percent above the minimum, they may be taxed.

Excess Aggregate Contributions

After-tax participant contributions or matching employer contributions that cause a plan to fail the 401(k) actual contribution percentage (ACP) non-discrimination test.

Excess Contributions

Pre-tax participant contributions that cause a plan to fail the 401(k) actual deferral percentage (ADP) non-discrimination test.

Excess Benefit Plan

A plan, or part of a plan, maintained to provide benefits that exceed IRS Code 415 limits on contributions and benefits.

Excludable Employees

The employees that may be excluded from the group being tested during 401(k) nondiscrimination testing. The following are excludable employees: certain ex-employees; certain airline pilots; non-resident aliens with no U.S. source of income; employees who do not meet minimum age and length of service requirements; and, employees whose retirement benefits are covered by collective bargaining agreements.

Exclusive Benefit Rule
A rule under ERISA that says the assets in an employee account may be used for the exclusive benefit of the employee and his/her beneficiaries.

Expense Ratio
The percentage of a fund's assets that are used to pay its annual expenses.

Facts and Circumstances Test
The test determining whether financial need exists for a 401(k) hardship withdrawal.

FICA
The Federal law that taxes employee wages for Social Security and other programs.

Fidelity Bond
Protects participants in the event a fiduciary or other responsible person steals or mishandles plan assets.

Fiduciary
A person with the authority to make decisions regarding a plan's assets or important administrative matters. Fiduciaries are required under ERISA to make decisions based solely on the best interests of plan participants.

Fiduciary Insurance
Insurance that protects plan fiduciaries in the event that they are found liable for a breach of fiduciary responsibility.

Forfeiture
Plan assets surrendered by participants upon termination of employment before being fully vested in the plan. Forfeitures may be distributed to the other participants in the plan or used to offset employer contributions.

Form 1099R
A form sent to the recipient of a plan distribution and filed with the IRS listing the amount of the distribution.

Form 5500
A form which all qualified retirement plans (excluding SEPs and SIMPLE IRAs) must file annually with the IRS.

Graduated or Graded Vesting

A vesting schedule in which the employee earns the right to employer contributions gradually over a period of years. For example, 25 percent ownership each year for four years. (See also *vesting*.)

Guaranteed Investment Contracts (GICs)

Accounts that are invested in interest-bearing contracts purchased directly from banks, insurance companies, or mutual funds, which guarantee to maintain the value of the principle and all accumulated interest. Also called stable value funds, these accounts do not go down in value.

Hardship or In-Service Distribution

When a participant withdraws plan funds prior to retirement, at the employer's option. Eligibility for such distributions exists when financial hardship is present. These distributions are taxable as early distributions and are subject to a ten percent early withdrawal federal income tax penalty if the participant is under age 59½.

Highly Compensated Employees (HCEs)

An employee who received more than $90,000 in compensation in 2002 (indexed annually) or is a 5 percent owner in the company.

Individually Directed Accounts

A brokerage account in a defined-contribution plan. Sometimes referred to as self-directed accounts.

Individual Retirement Account (IRA)

Personal retirement vehicles in which a person can make annual tax-deductible contributions. These accounts must meet IRS Code 408 requirements, but are created and funded at the discretion of the employee. They are not employer-sponsored plans.

Internal Revenue Service (IRS)

This branch of the U.S. Treasury Department is responsible for administering the requirements of qualified pension plans and other retirement vehicles. The IRS also worked with the DOL and the PWBC to develop Form 5500, and is now responsible for monitoring the data submitted annually on Form 5500 reports.

Keogh Plan
A qualified defined-contribution plan permitting self-employed individuals to contribute a portion of their earnings, pre-tax, to an individual account.

KSOP
A plan arrangement that includes both 401(k) contributions and an ESOP.

Leased Employee
An individual employed by a leasing organization that provides contractual services for the company for the period of more than one year.

Lump-Sum Distribution
The distribution at retirement of a participant's entire account balances within one calendar year due to retirement, death or disability.

Matching Contribution
A contribution made by the company to the account of the participant in ratio to contributions made by the participant.

Material Modification
A change in the terms of the plan that may affect plan participants, or other changes in a summary-plan document (SPD).

Median Market Cap
An indicator of the size of companies in which a fund invests.

Money-Market Fund
A mutual fund seeking to generate income for participants through investments in short-term securities.

Money-Purchase Plan
A type of defined-contribution plan in which the employer's contributions are determined by a specific formula, usually as a percentage of pay. Contributions are not dependent on company profits.

Multi-Employer Plan
A pension plan to which more than one employer contributes, and which is maintained according to collective bargaining agreements.

Mutual Fund
An account with a broad range of investment options, each of which are diversified, reducing the risk to the participant.

Named Fiduciary
The plan document must name one or more fiduciaries, giving them the authority to control and manage the operation of the plan. The named fiduciary must also be identified as a fiduciary by a procedure specified in the plan document.

Nondiscrimination Rules
IRS rules that prohibit the plan or plan sponsor from giving disproportionately larger benefits to highly compensated employees (HCEs). Specific nondiscimination testing must be done to determine if plans have broken this rule and are top heavy.

Nonelective Contribution
An employer contribution that cannot be withdrawn or paid to the employee in cash. This contribution is neither a matching contribution, nor an elective contribution.

Non-Highly Compensated Employees (NHCEs)
Employees who are not highly compensated. Generally, they are employees who earned less than $90,000 in 2002 (indexed for inflation). See *highly compensated employees*.

Non-Qualified Deferred Compensation Plan
A plan subject to tax, in which the assets of certain employees (usually highly compensated employees) are deferred. These funds may be accessed by an employer's creditors.

Open-Architecture Service Providers
Previously referred to as bundled providers, an open-architecture firm generally provides one or two of the five necessary services mentioned in this book. Unbundled providers traditionally place an emphasis on their record-keeping administration, compliance, and consulting.

Outsourcing
A defined-contribution plan term not to be confused with total-benefits outsourcing. This terms means the record-keeping service provider is handling all participant inquiries and transactions, including the approval of distributions, loans, and withdrawals, but does not include providing legal services.

Participant
Person who has an account in the plan and any beneficiaries who may be eligible to receive an account balance.

Participant-Directed Account
A plan that allows participants to select their own investment options from the plan sponsor's fund menu.

Party-in-Interest
Those who are a party-in-interest to a plan include: the employer; the directors, officers, employees or owners of the employer; any employee organization whose members are plan participants; plan fiduciaries; and plan service providers.

Passive Management
The style of a professional investment or mutual-fund manager who believes that purchasing all stocks of a sector of the market is the key to a successful fund. The opposite is active management whereby the professional believes that stock picking and market timing are the keys to a successful fund.

Pension and Welfare Benefits Administration (PWBA)
This branch of the Department of Labor protects the pensions, health plans, and other employee benefits of American workers. The PWBA enforces Title I of ERISA, which contains rules for reporting and disclosure, vesting, participation, funding, and fiduciary conduct.

Pension Benefit Guaranty Corporation (PBGC)
A federal agency established by Title IV of ERISA for the insurance of defined benefit pension plans. The PBGC provides payment of pension benefits if a plan terminates and is unable to cover all required benefits.

Plan Administrator
The individual, group or corporation named in the plan document as responsible for day-to-day operations. The plan sponsor is generally the plan administrator if no other entity is named.

Plan Document
The parameters under which a retirement plan will be operated must be outlined in the plan document. This document must be given to employees upon request.

Plan Loan
Loan from a participant's accumulated plan assets, not to exceed 50 percent of the balance, or $50,000, less the amount of any outstanding loans. This is an optional plan feature.

Plan Sponsor
The entity responsible for establishing and maintaining the plan.

Plan Year
The calendar, policy or fiscal year for which plan records are maintained.

Portability
This occurs when, upon termination of employment, an employee transfers pension funds from one employer's plan, to another, without penalty.

Pre-Retirement Survivor Rights
The right of a surviving beneficiary to receive benefits if vested plan participant dies before retirement.

Price/Book Ratio
The share price of a stock divided by its net worth, or book value, per share.

Price/Earnings (PE) Ratio
The ratio of a stock's current price to its earnings per share over the past year. The PE ratio of a fund is the weighted average of the PE ratios of the stocks it holds.

Prohibited Transaction
Activities regarding treatment of plan assets by fiduciaries that are prohibited by ERISA. This includes transactions with a party-in-interest, including sale, exchange, lease, or loan of plan securities or other properties.

Profit-Sharing Plan
Company-sponsored plan funded only by company contributions. Company contributions may be determined by a fixed formula related to the employer's profits, or may be at the discretion of the board of directors.

Prudent Man Rule
ERISA fiduciary law that requires all fiduciaries to conduct the business of the plan with prudence and care. Any fiduciary violating this law is liable to the plan and its participants for all losses.

Qualified Domestic Relations Order (QDRO)
A judgment, decree or order that creates or recognizes an alternate payee's (such as former spouse, child, etc.) right to receive all, or a portion, of a participant's retirement plan benefits.

Qualified Joint and Survivor Annuity (QJSA)
An annuity with payments continuing to the surviving spouse after the participant's death, equal to at least 50 percent of the participant's benefit.

Qualified Plan
Any plan that qualifies for favorable tax treatment by meeting the requirements of section 401(a) of the Internal Revenue Code and by following applicable regulations. Includes 401(k) and deferred profit-sharing plans.

Record-Keeping Service Provider
A firm that provides a plan sponsor, record-keeping administration and compliance services.

Request For Proposal (RFP)
A questionnaire sent to vendors soliciting a bid for their services. The questionnaire generally focuses on pricing, service capabilities, business model, and current client statistics.

Rollover
The action of moving plan assets from one qualified plan to another, or to an IRA within 60 days of distributions, while retaining the tax benefits of a qualified plan.

Sacred Cows
Processes that have not been changed for years because that is the way the company is used to processing. These processes if changed, generally lead to better service to the customer and more efficient internal processing.

Same Day/Late Day Trading
A term used in defined-contribution plans for describing a type of daily valuation plan. It means that all trades across multiple mutual-fund families will occur at the same price, but it is technically not processed at the mutual-fund company until late that evening. Record-keeping service providers have the ability to update participants' accounts before the trades actually occur.

Safe Harbor Rules
Provisions that exempt certain individuals or kinds of companies from one or more regulations.

Salary Deduction
Also known as payroll deduction. When a plan participant arranges to have pre-tax contributions made directly from their paycheck, it is arranged through salary deduction.

Savings Incentive Match Plan for Employees (SIMPLE)
A type of defined-contribution plan for employers with 100 or fewer employees, in which the employer matches employee deferrals up to 3 percent of compensation, or provides non-elective contributions up to 2 percent of compensation. These contributions are immediately and 100 percent vested, and they are the only employer contribution to the plan. SIMPLE plans may be structured as individual retirement accounts (IRAs) or as 401(k) plans.

Service Provider
A company that provides any type of service to the plan, including managing assets, record keeping, providing plan education, and administering the plan.

Schedule SSA
A form that must be filed by all plans subject to ERISA Section 203 minimum vesting requirements. The schedule, which is attached to Form 5500, provides data on participants who separated from service with a vested benefit but were not paid their benefits.

Shareholder Service Fee
A fee paid from a mutual-fund company to a directed trustee or clearing firm.

Simplified Employee-Pension Plan (SEP)
A defined-contribution plan in which employers make contributions to individual employee accounts (similar to IRAs). Employees may also make pre-tax contributions to these accounts. As of January 1997, no new SEP plans may be formed.

SIMPLE Plan
See *Savings Incentive Match Plan for Employees.*

Stable-Value Fund
A conservative fund consisting of GIC contracts and synthetics. Very popular in the defined benefit and defined-contribution plans.

Stock Bonus Plan
A defined-contribution plan in which company contributions are distributable in the form of company stock.

Sub-TA
A fee generally paid by mutual fund companies to record-keeping service providers for providing sub transfer agent type services. This simply means the mutual fund has one record on file by plan, as opposed to one record for every participant in the plan. The record-keeping service provider tracks the accounts by participant.

Summary Annual Report
A report that companies must file annually on the financial status of the plan. The summary annual report must be automatically provided to participants every year.

Summary Plan Description (SPD)
A document describing the features of an employer-sponsored plan. The primary purpose of the SPD is to disclose the features of the plan to current and potential plan participants. ERISA requires that certain information be contained in the SPD, including participant rights under ERISA, claims procedures and funding arrangements.

Summary of Material Modifications
A document that must be distributed to plan participants summarizing any material modifications made to a plan.

Target-Benefit Plan
A type of defined-contribution plan in which company contributions are based on an actuarial valuation designed to provide a target benefit to each participant upon retirement. The plan does not guarantee that such benefit will be paid; its only obligation is to pay whatever benefit can be provided by the amount in the participant's account. It is a hybrid of a money-purchase plan and a defined-benefit plan.

Tax-Sheltered Annuity (TSA)
See *403(b) plan.*

Third Party Administrator (TPA)
These firms only perform the compliance function. Although many in the industry use this term loosely, these firms do not perform the day-to-day record-keeping administration of updating participants' accounts. In addition, the acronym TPA is often used in the health care sector of employee-benefit plans, and can be confusing to the plan sponsor.

Top-Heavy Plan
A plan in which 60 percent of account balances (both vested and non-vested) are held by certain highly compensated employees.

Total Benefits Outsourcing
Outsourcing in which the service provider handles all defined-contribution, defined benefit, and health and welfare services for the plan sponsor and participant; but, does not include legal work or claims processing for health and dental claims (although some firms do include this). The participant goes to one site or service provider for all benefit transactions and inquiries.

Trustee
The bank or trust company that has the responsibility for holding plan assets. (Please see definitions for discretionary and directed trustees.) It is also the person or entity that has fiduciary responsibility for the plan.

Turnover Rate (of a fund)
A measure of the trading activity in a mutual fund.

Vesting
The participants' ownership right to company contributions. Typically these are graded over a period of time up to five years. For example, if you are 50% vested in your plan's company contributions, simply multiply the company contribution account by 50%, and that is your vested balance.

Vesting Schedule
The structure for determining participants' ownership right to company contributions (see *matching contribution*). In a plan with immediate vesting, partic-

ipants own all company contributions as soon as they are deposited into individual accounts. In cliff vesting, company contributions will be fully owned (i.e., vested) only after a specific amount of time, and employees leaving before the allotted time are not entitled to any company contributions (with certain exceptions for retirees). In plans with graduated or graded vesting, vesting occurs in specified increments.

Sample RFP Start-Up Kit
Standard Defined Contribution Plan

Recordkeeping Service Provider Search Tips

The keys to hiring a new recordkeeping service provider are to make sure you are in control of the process and to not allow the service providers to sell you a solution that fits their strengths, as opposed to the needs of your company and culture. Here are a few guidelines to follow:

- Design your optimal plan before sending the RFP or interviewing candidates.
- Do not send courtesy RFPs, as the recordkeeping service provider or advisor will spend a lot of time completing the RFP.
- Provide service provider candidates a complete history of your plan and your desired traits for successful service providers (this can be highlighted in the cover letter). Include a copy of last year's Form 5500, plan document, SPD, and sample participant communications.
- Be honest with the recordkeeping service providers throughout the process. If they do not make the cut for an RFP, finalist presentation, or winner, tell them straight out.
- Keep the RFP short and concise, and eliminate questions that really do not tell you anything about the provider. Remember, you have to read the answers and you will find that a lot of the answers are sales fluff.
- Send a cover letter with the RFP timeline, and stick to it. It is best to build in extra time for each phase of the RFP:

- Review of RFPs
- Finalist Presentations
- Selecting Providers

- Do not take sales calls during the process under the guise of additional questions. Simply set up one day within the first week after sending out the RFP to conduct 20-minute phone calls with each of the service providers. On the cover letter, provide a contact name to schedule the 20-minute phone call, with times filled on a first come, first serve basis. This is the fairest way to get to know the service providers and allows them to ask questions and start the sales process. Plus, it will eliminate a lot of calls during the process, and believe me, if you do not do this, you will get at least 2-3 calls a day.

- Spend an hour or two with an established unbiased consultant (not an investment advisor/broker) to discuss the state of defined contribution service providers. They will tell you the inside story of how every provider gets paid and their strengths/weaknesses. They can also provide you a list of best recordkeeping service provider candidates based on your criteria.

- The two most important components of the success of a DC plan are communications and investments.

- Watch out for hidden fees or high investment expenses. Focusing solely on out-of-pocket fees may look great for your firm at the expense of the participant, and can lead to future litigation. You have the option to charge administration fees against the trust, and hence to focus on the total fees.

The following are sample questions that we use to screen candidates. Our goal is to receive substantive information as well as to protect you from future issues and liabilities related to over-promising during the sales process.

General

1. Please provide names, addresses, telephone and fax numbers as well as e-mail addresses of individuals responsible for responding to the RFP. If an investment advisor or broker is responding with a recordkeeping service provider, please provide information for both the advisor and the recordkeeping service for this question and throughout entire section.

2. Provide a brief history of your company's services with respect to defined contribution plan administration/recordkeeping, compliance, investment management and/or trustee services including:

- Your target market
- Length of time services have been provided
- Emphasis on your competitive advantages

3. How many people does your company employ in total and by responsibility area? What percentage of firm revenue accounts for Defined Contribution administration?

4. Do you have experience with clients who have acquired companies/plans? What role did you play and what are some of the issues a plan sponsor should think about before an acquisition?

5. Please provide a chart indicating the number of daily valued participant directed plans and other valuations.

Number of Employees	Daily Valuation	Other Valuations (monthly/quarterly)
Under 100		
100-499		
500-999		
1,000-4,999		
Over 5,000		
Total		

6. From what office would your organization administer (recordkeeping, administration) all services? Tell us about your customer service approach at the plan sponsor and participant level.

DWC Notes About the Team

Overall, distinguishing between recordkeepers does not necessarily come down to just technology. An important, but often overlooked, factor is the processing team. Any service provider can buy or create a great system, but do they have the talent to run the process? Ask your finalist to introduce you to the full processing team — including the day-to-day processor and the day-to-day manager. Ask these individuals what a typical day is like; this will tell you a lot about staffing and planning. Each service provider has different hiring characteristics for all levels. Do not be afraid to ask what their criteria are. Finally, ask your finalist to specifically describe their training process. Does the service provider have an in-depth training program for new hires or new managers? Training is important; do not overlook the value of continued training, especially as it relates to compliance issues. An important point to remember is that recordkeeping administrators have a turnover percentage close to 50% annually.

7. Do you have the capability within your company, or through alliances, to provide the full range of services desired by ABC COMPANY (administration, recordkeeping, compliance, trustee, custodial, communications and investment management of plan assets)? Indicate the services that would be provided by an alliance partner and a brief history of your relationship with such partner.

Systems

When creating this section and the next one related to recordkeeping administration, the key is to determine what distinguishes the recordkeeping service providers.

1. Flexibility in plan design and investment selection

2. The ability to quarterback the process — investment managers, trustee, recordkeeping systems and your payroll all linked to the system.

3. Participant should have easy access to the service provider and be able to get results fast, preferably through a strong IVR System/Call Center and Internet. Key factors are:
   - Easy to follow system.
   - Speed of systems response. Does the system answer on the first ring for opt outs (assuming the recordkeeping service provider offers a Call Center)? Is the Internet site responsive?
   - Low percentage of calls not answered by the Customer Service Representative or that receives a busy signal, alternatively are on hold a long time. Opt-outs can include internet chat sessions as well.

- Customer Service Representatives (Call Center or Internet Chat Sessions)— What is their background and capacity? Also, what hours are they available? Do they have customized screens for each plan?
- Can the system be programmed for your plan?
- Can the system handle share or unit accounting (whichever you select) in a true daily environment? Unit accounting may apply to separately managed accounts.
- Ability to store investment fund performance and provide on demand.
- Ability to handle loan modeling with more than one payroll source. Can the system handle note-less loans?
- Utilizes bar coding and other technology for return transactions such as enrollments, loans, and withdrawals.
- Can the system take salary deferral changes?
- Does the recordkeeper link with your payroll provider, in your format, for sending contributions and loan repayments, indicative information and participant status codes?
- Can the system handle all vesting schedules and perform the tracking from your payroll data?
- Can the system perform eligibility calculations and coordinate enrollment packages to newly eligible participants?

NOTE: The best time to test a service provider's voice response system and Internet speed is between 11:00 a.m. to 2:00 p.m., as this is when the system is most frequently utilized.

4. Ability to provide proactive service in relation to plan issues, such as non-discrimination testing, planning, and reporting. Ask for a copy of the non-discrimination test that they provide to their current customers. Is the report user friendly, and is it accompanied with an explanation letter, or is the report a bunch of numbers with a test result?

5. Provides plan sponsor with user-friendly reports, including quarterly management reports and recordkeeping reports. Find out if these reports are customizable and, if so, what is the cost. Review these reports before hiring a recordkeeper.

6. Can the recordkeeping system handle any transfer restrictions, equity wash, multiple funds, multiple plans, transfer method, and withdrawal provisions? Ask for examples of other plans with similar restrictions and call the references.

7. What are the internal proof and controls? Have the finalist provide specific examples of used proof and control sheets for one day in each of the last six months. When are trust-to-records reconciliations provided to the client? Can you request them daily if you want to?

8. Go onsite to see if they track daily transaction statistics for timeliness and accuracy. If they do not, are they really managing the process?

9. Does the recordkeeper have a true disaster recovery program in place? Make sure it is more than 20 minutes.

10. Is there a completed SAS70 Level II audit on all of the recordkeeper's procedures? In addition, ask who completed it and how much of the audit was performed in house.

11. Can the recordkeeper operate in a true daily environment? In today's environment, true daily (Same day/Late day) recordkeeping should be a standard practice, including separately managed funds.

Need heading here/don't understand break

1. Please provide the software you use for the following components. If you are using an alliance partner, please include their software.
    *   Recordkeeping Administration
    *   Compliance
    *   Form 5500
    *   Trust Reporting
    *   Investment Performance
    *   Investment Selection

2. Will ABC COMPANY have online access to the defined contribution system (i.e., participant recordkeeping, and trust)?

3. Describe your hardware environment.

4. How often do you enhance and upgrade your software? When is the next scheduled upgrade?

5. Describe how your system handles mass changes or global updates that may result from plan acquisitions or changes in ERISA code.

6. Do you have a completed SAS70 for recordkeeping and trust systems and operations? Is the SAS70 a Level II?

7. Do you have full disaster recovery capabilities for up to 48 hours for all systems?

8. Is the directed trustee/clearing function integrated with the recordkeeping system? Is it straight through processing? Please Describe.

Plan Administration/Recordkeeping

1. Describe your Internet access for participant inquiry and transactions? Do you offer push technology or opt-out to Customer Service Representatives for online users? If so, could you provide us with a sample account number and password?

2. Do you have a Call Center with Customer Service Representatives? If so, please provide available hours. Is your Call Center fulfillment on-site? Briefly describe your competitive advantages as to why our participants will be satisfied with your Call Center.

3. Do you have same-day/late-day trading capabilities? If so, please list eligible funds.

4. Do you provide service guarantees for your performance? If so, please list standard guarantees.

5. If you make an error, will you or your partners make the plan whole? Please address the following areas:
   - Participant Recordkeeping (timeliness or inaccurate)
   - Compliance Testing (timing or inaccurate)
   - Form 5500 Completion
   - Plan Document or SPD

6. Describe the capabilities of your system and/or process to support the following:
   - Eligibility and proper entry date
   - Participant account inquiry
   - Investment changes and elections
   - Limiting participant elective deferrals to 402(g) limits
   - Participant loan administration (provide a process of a typical loan transaction describing the roll of each party, timing of check, paperless loans, loan data provided, standard format of reporting)
   - Calculation of federal withholding
   - Track and calculate age 70½ minimum distributions
   - Separate tracking of HCEs to limit deferrals to the 401(k) plan
   - 1 –5 year graded vesting scale
   - Withdrawals/Distributions (timeliness of check, eligibility for hardships: who makes final approval, forms and confirmations provided to participants)
   - Compliance Tests
   - Payroll Interface
   - Plan Documents
   - SPD's

DWC Notes: Compliance Testing

Every recordkeeping service provider has the capability to perform all of the required tests; however, your due diligence should focus on the following:
   - What level of employee performs the tests and reviews them? Is there a dedicated group, or does the processing team perform?
   - Are the tests performed from the recordkeeping system, compliance only software, or spreadsheets? (You might be surprised at how many firms use the latter for testing.)
   - Who actually signs off on the test, the recordkeeping service provider or the plan sponsor? Some firms actually ask the plan sponsor to sign off on the test.)
   - What is the standard turnaround on projected and final tests? Will they guarantee the turnaround time?

- Do they require year-end input in a special format, even though they store the data on the system?
- Who tracks HCE's?
- How many of the Form 5500's are extended?
- Do they perform Financial Summaries?

The bottom line is to interview the personal who will be performing the tests and ask for performance statistics (accuracy and timing).

7. What is your recommended method of initial enrollment for the ABC COMPANY? Is it mapping or a one-time election in advance of the conversion date? What is the ongoing method of enrollment (i.e., paper, VRU, Internet, etc.)?

8. Briefly describe the valuation process and schedule for a client with daily valuation. Discuss daily transfers from the participant's viewpoint, and contribution processing for the plan sponsor's standpoint.

9. Describe the reconciliation process between plan, trust, and payroll.

DWC Notes on the Trustee/Custodian

A trustee plays an important role in the recordkeeping process only for unbundled players, particularly in daily valuation environments. The mutual fund companies generally use one system for recordkeeping and extract an annual report as they can clear their own trades. Recordkeeping Only (unbundled) firms require a directed trustee (or custodian) to trade mutual funds on behalf of the plan and participant.

If you are selecting an unbundled service provider, you must rate their directed trustee as well; do not take their partnership as a given, as often the recordkeeping service provider has selected the low cost provider that does not have unlimited liability for trades not processed on time or in error. Research all of the following via the directed trustee direct and/or the day-to-day recordkeepers, as the sales team and managers will say everything is seamless and truly linked:

- The established link between the trustee, custodian and the recordkeeping system. Are all processes truly electronic?
- Turnaround time on check processing.

- Is the annual report easy to read? A clean annual report will keep your external audit fees to a minimum.

- Can the bundled service achieve same day/late day trading across all mutual fund families and separately managed funds? Are they linked with the NSCC? Do they offer IDA's?

- If the recordkeeping service provider includes the directed trustee fees in their overall fees (meaning they do not break out the directed trustee fees), make sure you ask.

- Does the directed trustee require certain funds for lower fees, such as money market funds or Stable Value Funds? You simply want this answer for due diligence, as the answer may be yes, and it is crucial to know this to prevent future litigation. Especially in the case of a fund performing far below standards with high expense ratios.

- Who receives float from distribution checks or contributions wired but not invested? Find out.

- What systems do they use for clearing, trust, and check cutting? Some directed trustees do not use traditional trust systems, as they are only providing clearing services.

- Does the directed trustee pay for all of their trading errors, timing and accuracy? Some directed trustees limit liability to a dollar amount or a multiple of their fee from the plan sponsor.

10. If applicable, outline how you interface with your alliance partners to provide any aspects of your administration, disbursement services, trustee services, etc.

11. How often do you send paper participant statements? What is your standard turnaround time? Can the statements be customized? Please provide an example.

12. Please indicate the type of historical plan information you maintain on participants. How often do you update your files? For how long, and where, is information stored and maintained? Who has the rights to the plan information in your standard contract?

13. How are fund transfer entries checked for completeness and accuracy before the transaction is completed and confirmed?

14. What reporting does the plan sponsor receive, by what mediums, how often, and what is the level of flexibility?

DWC Notes: Plan Sponsor Report Access

Finally, with technology improvements, online access is becoming easier for plans to receive reports in a format that is easy to read. The best-of-class systems allow for ad-hoc report creation as an option for employees and the plan sponsor, commonly referred to as report writers. These tools are convenient to have in the HR office, but in an outsourced environment, the goal is to get the employee to use the 1-800 line or the Internet for all questions. Companies requesting a lot of ad-hoc reports will want to hire a recordkeeper that can program these quickly and incorporate them into the standard reports, thus minimizing HR's online access needs.

The bottom line: Ad-hoc reports and report writers are fantastic features, but should never be used as key criteria in selecting a recordkeeper. You should always rate recordkeeping service providers by their ability to satisfy the participant through IVR, Internet and participant statements. If it is a toss up between service providers in relation to serving the participant, compliance capabilities may be a good tiebreaker.

Communications

1. Based on our demographics, provide information on the standard communication campaign that you would provide us.

2. Can the participant at anytime determine his/her realistic retirement goals? If so, please describe.

3. Can the participant determine the best asset allocation for their needs, at any time? If so, please describe.

4. What level of customization can you provide?

5. Please enclose copies of standard written communications and links to online information.

6. Can the participant receive direct one-on-one advice?

Tips

- We are advocates for recordkeeping service providers and their partners providing substantive one-on-one sessions, on-site or through the Internet.
- Paper communications and on-site meetings are often expensive in real dollars, especially on-site communications in time away from the job, if performed during normal business hours. Make sure on-site meetings are performed by a professional with experience and will provide an entertaining and substantive session. Interview the professional during the final presentation
- Leverage the Internet! Everyone has access to a computer in today's world. Worst case, is to purchase/rent a PC as a kiosk in the offices or breakroom.
- Design a campaign for your plan and understand that the success of the plan (participation rates or value) starts with your senior management and influencers, NOT the service provider.

Investments

1. In your opinion, what does the ideal plan look like from an investment perspective, such as number of funds, type of funds, and strategy? Provide us with your optimal investment package, one that best allows each of our participants to reach their goals. (Please do not worry about our philosophy or culture, as we are interested in what you believe will be successful for a typical defined contribution plan.)

2. Our current investment menu offers funds our Committee wants to keep with the new provider, (list them here). Can you accommodate these funds, and how does it impact the fees or participant communication process?

3. Are IDA's available?

4. Are there any added fees other than the investment manager's fund expenses? Are there any front end or back end loads? Do you have any surrender fees?

5. If the funds include sub-TA's, 12b-1's, or dealer concessions, please identify the amounts and who is receiving.

6. Will you provide investment policy and monitoring services?

7. Referencing your answer to question 1 above, please provide a mapping solution for the conversion for funds you recommend we replace (of course funds that remain from the current menu will not be mapped).

Tips

- Our ideal plan includes LifeStyle Funds, 4-12 traditional funds, and an online brokerage solution.
- The investment menu is only as strong as your communication campaign
- An online brokerage solution is not right for every plan; however, if your plan has a "know-it-all" participant who is not happy with any investment fund choice, this is an excellent option. We recommend they sign a waiver that acknowledges they are responsible for the actions (without implying the plan takes full responsibility if they do not sign). This is a tricky one; however, we have standard documents.
- The answer to question 5 will reveal quite a bit, and if an investment advisor is involved, it is crucial to obtain a letter of engagement from the advisor acknowledging how much h/she will get paid and for what services.

Fees

Based on information provided, please provide us your annual fee estimates in an easy-to-read format. You can provide your fee schedule as an addendum; however, we are interested in making this process easy for all parties. Specifically, break out your fees into the following components:

- Recordkeeping Administration (if you have transaction costs, provide us the fee for the transaction, and assume industry standards for transaction counts)
- Trustee/Custodian
- Communications
- Compliance
- Investment Advisory (you do not need to include mutual fund expense ratios, only added fees you may charge)
- Conversion
- Surrender or termination fees

After receipt, which we expect to see as one annual number (excluding conversion), we will compare all service providers on an even comparison including investment fund expenses (we will map funds for comparison purposes, and default to your highest expense ratio fund or what you instruct us to map to). Specifically stated, we will assume the same number of transactions for a given transaction if more than one firm charges a transaction fee for that category.

How does one compare fees between the providers and get a true "Apples to Apples" comparison?

For starters, nothing is free. If it looks too good to be true, it probably is. Having said that, your plan may receive a very low recordkeeping administration bid or close to nothing if you have asset power. The most important rule of thumb when reviewing fees is to not focus on the recordkeeping portion only. Often plan sponsors look only at this fee, as this is the fee they have to pay (although plans have the option of charging fees to the trust). Let's put this in perspective, and compare two recordkeeping bids for a plan with $5 million in assets. Following are the respective bids with the assumption that the services are equal:

	Annual Recordkeeping Fees
Service Provider A	$10,000
Service Provider B	$ 0

All services being equal, it seems like a no-brainer to select Service Provider B. However, let's compare the average investment expenses (assumption of 60% in Equities and 40% in Fixed). To continue to make comparison easy, the two providers have the same investment portfolio return (therefore the difference to the participant in annual return is the difference in fees):

	Average Investment Expense	Annual Investment Expenses
Service Provider A	75 basis points (.75%)	$37,500
Service Provider B	150 basis point (1.5%)	$75,000

Again, it would appear to be a no-brainer to select Service Provider A, as participants would receive .75% more in earnings each year, let alone the compounding effect. In this straightforward example, the plan would be much better off if they charged the recordkeeping fees against the plan, as the participants are still better off in the short and long term.

Obviously, the comparisons are actually more complex, as each service provider will provide an array of funds. In order to rate service providers on an "Apples to Apples" comparison, you will need to have the funds selected during the review process. What really makes this difficult is the fact that no one can predict the future return of any fund. There is an old axiom in the industry: "Any investor will pay a higher investment fee when the performance is higher." Less subtly, an investor will pay an annual expense of 1.5% for a 20% past return as compared to 1% for a past 10% return (assuming the funds are in the same class). Before digressing too far, risk obviously plays a component, therefore, the longer the time horizon for comparison of funds, the better.

Back to the task at hand, the pricing model takes a whole new twist or added layer. In the above example, Service Provider B was clearly subsidized from the investment funds for its recordkeeping expense. Coming from the recordkeeper's perspective, what is really scary is that approximately 90% of the work related to the plan is performed by the recordkeeper and, in most cases, the recordkeepers are the ones that have to sharpen the pencil in the bidding process. Simply stated, 90% of the overall plan equates to a small percentage of the total fees associated with the plan. Obviously, these percentages change based on the size of the plan in terms of assets, but the ratio will be tilted heavily to the investment fund expenses. This will be true for bundled or unbundled service providers.

Bundled service providers have a built in advantage in bidding fees, as they can clearly bundle all services under one fee umbrella. Unbundled service providers can offer funds that pay revenue sharing from the built-in investment management fee from the mutual funds. These revenue sharing components can come from shareholder service fees or sub-TA fees. Depending on whether a broker or advisor is involved, 12b-1 fees may be available for revenue sharing as well. These service providers pass back to the plan sponsor revenue sharing devised from the agreements either in a direct or indirect offset. Direct offsets are the best answer in order for the client to understand and know all of the fee arrangements. The mutual funds have become very aggressive in their dealings with recordkeepers. There is more revenue sharing money available today than there was one year ago, as fund families recognize the major distribution channels through recordkeepers and trustees/custodians (discussed in the trustees/custodian section). Fund families typically offer up to 25-50 basis points through 12b-1's, sub-accounting or sub-transfer agent fees and shareholder service fees. Some funds even pay one-time finders' fees (ranging from twenty-five to one hundred basis points).

References/Closing

1. We will not request references until we have reached final negotiations. If you feel it necessary to provide references that might be applicable in advance, we will call them.

2. Do you represent that all questions have been answered accurately and agree that all answers will be incorporated as addendum to the service contract? (We understand the fees may change based on further discussions.)

3. Please provide a copy of your standard contract.

4. Will you recognize your role as a co-fiduciary? Will you recognize any role as a co-fiduciary?

DWC Notes: References and Compatibility with other EB Services

For middle market plans, total outsourcing of benefits, including health and welfare processing, is becoming price competitive. If your service provider does not provide these capabilities, you may end up with multiple systems and toll free numbers down the road. One 1-800 number and Internet site for all employee benefit services is an excellent feature for your participants and your HR staff. Eliminating HR activity in the annual re-enrollment process is becoming commonplace. The first place a company looks is at the service provider who performs the defined contribution administration or the payroll provider.

A rule of thumb used in hiring a service provider in the defined contribution industry is asking for specific references related to plans of your size.

Do not be afraid to ask for the entire client list to see if you know anybody else using the recordkeeping firm. If flexibility is important, the participant statements, IVR system, and recordkeeping system report examples are a good indication of the amount of flexibility this service provider can handle. Don't forget that a majority of references are known references and sometimes partners. Having said that, roughly 5% of references turn out to be negative. This, of course, will immediately put the brakes on that provider.

Contact Information
Keith Clark
Direct Line: 952-832-5864
E-Mail: kclark@dwcconsultants.com

Sample RFP Kit for Directed Trustees

(For directed trustees on behalf of the Recordkeeping Service Provider)

Overview

1. Please provide a history of your organization and how directed trustee services fit into the overall business plan.

2. What is your target market for directed trustee services? Discuss your growth in the last two years.

3. Provide us a background on your market presence:
   - Number of defined contribution plans (daily and non-daily segregated)
   - Total Assets (defined contribution only)
   - Number of recordkeeping service provider clients with at least 10 plans or more
   - Total Assets and number of plans served in your largest recordkeeping service provider client

4. Provide us your service guarantees and your standard contract with recordkeeeping service providers.

5. Do you place any maximums on liability such as a multiple or percentage of the plan sponsor fee?

6. Will you incorporate all of your answers from this RFI into our contract?

7. How many employees serve the directed trustee line of business? How many levels of employees do you have (day-to-day, manager, senior manager, etc)? What is your training program and budget per person? How are employees motivated? How is growth of clients anticipated?

8. Describe your Quality Assurance Program. How do you measure quality? Please include your SAS70 report.

Systems/Service

Please address the following:

- Systems used to serve the recordkeeping service provider and client
    1. Trustee System
    2. Check Writing
    3. Online Capabilities
    4. Clearing

- How to integrate the following tasks
    1. Daily Pricing (when and how) (please bear in mind we currently process in the evening)
    2. Next Day Reconciliations
    3. Distribution Flow/Check Writing
    4. Contribution Flow (include timing)
    5. Loans Granted (how do you track loans?)
    6. New Business Set-Up (identify all roles, responsibilities, mandatory forms, and timing)
    7. Transitioning Business due to lost clients

- Describe your online Capabilities at the recordkeeping service provider or plan sponsor level
- Describe your service team approach, on a macro basis, and how you may set up the service team for us
- Describe your trust reporting process. Who gets reports and when? Are the annual reports certified? Provide examples.

Pricing/Revenue Sharing

Please address the following:

- Plan Fees, and address each of the scenarios below by including fees, asset based and transactions. If you have transaction fees and the transaction is not included in our estimates below, use your estimates based on your experience (you may leverage a money market or Stable Value Fund Solution)

- – Start Up Plan with 25 participants and bi-weekly payroll, and 3 checks during the year (and 2 ACH)
- – $500,000 Plan with 25 participants and weekly payroll (5 checks)
- – $2 million Plan with 100 participants and weekly payroll and 20 checks
- – General Pricing (please include any minimums)

- Relationship Pricing
- When do you invoice and are you flexible on the timing? Is invoicing in arrears or forward?

From a revenue sharing perspective, please address the Revenue Sharing component. Provide a complete fund list available to our clients and include all shareholder service fees and sub-TA's you will collect for us. If you take a cut, provide us this amount. Describe the process. For mutual funds that pay based on participant count, how do you work with us to collect the sub-TA's?

Please disclose any soft dollar arrangements in your pricing, if any (not including float). If you are accepting marketing fees for any fund families, please disclose those as well.

References

We will request references upon completion of the initial due diligence phase. Our preference is three references with the following characteristics:

- Similar size to us (insert your name)
- A client that has been with you longer than 2 years
- A client that has started working with you within the last 6 months

DWC Consultants Business Creed

Our Code of Ethics

- We will perform our services at the highest level of ethical standards, period. We will set the highest level of ethical standards, which includes:
    1. Straight forward service contracts that clearly outline our responsibilities, including service guarantees
    2. Taking 100% responsibility (including fiduciary responsibility where applicable)
    3. Disclosure of all revenue to our clients and accept no softdollars or marketing fees
    4. We will always tell the truth in every endeavor and we will never misrepresent our services and abilities

- We will treat our team members, clients, friends of the firm, and vendors in a manner in which we want to be treated ourselves; honestly with full disclosure and proactive open communications.

- We will use person to person discussions when discussing any negative or time sensitive issues, and will not send these types of messages via email or voicemail

- Confidential information will remain confidential

- We will report any unlawful practices to the appropriate authorities. We will openly discuss any situations with the appropriate parties which our firm, industry, and/or community would deem unethical. We will not engage or work with firms that we deem practice unethically (as deemed by us).

- We will hire team members based solely on their ability and offer equal employment regardless of race, religion, ethnic group, sexual orientation, or sex.

- We will hire our service providers and vendors based on their abilities and price solely, and will not accept kickbacks, soft dollars, or quid pro quos. Furthermore, we will not accept gifts from non-clients, such as vendors, service providers that we rate and review, and friends of the firm.

- We will take a leadership role in the communities in which we work and live, through charitable contributions and donating time, specifically we will dedicate at least 5% of our direct revenue and 5% of our time.

About DWC Consultants, Inc.

DWC Consultants, Inc., founded in 1999 by Keith Clark, is an employee-benefits consulting firm with expertise in disciplines such as Defined Contribution, Defined Benefit, Executive Compensation, Health & Welfare, Communications, and General HR Consulting. Located in Minneapolis, Minnesota, the DWC Strategy Group provides consulting and strategy services to financial service firms with an emphasis on Best Practice/Operations, Cost Benefit Analysis/Pricing, Marketing and Sales Strategies.

The DWC Client Service Group provides companies with employee-benefits solutions ranging from selecting and implementing the best administration solution through providing traditional consulting services including plan design, participant communications, and voluntary compliance audits.

Keith H. Clark, Jr., *Consultant*

Keith Clark has over 16 years of employee-benefits consulting experience, with an emphasis on record-keeping administration, plan consulting, investments, and trust reporting. Keith is a frequent speaker and writer, and was named one of the top 401(k) consultants by Pension Management Magazine in December of 1995.

Nevin E. Adams

Nevin is Executive Editor of **PLAN SPONSOR** magazine and its Web counterpart, **PLANSPONSOR.com**, the nation's leading authority on pension and retirement issues. He also writes and publishes PLANSPONSOR.com's **NewsDash**, a daily email update focused on the critical issues impacting benefits industry professionals.

A 24-year veteran of the retirement services industry, he has held senior positions at both Wachovia Bank and Northern Trust, dealing with both pension and defined contribution issues, while working directly with employers on a daily basis.

A frequent speaker at industry and trade conferences, he graduated magna cum laude with a BS in Finance, as well as a JD from DePaul University in Chicago, Illinois. He is also on the Advisory Board for the Certified Retirement Services Professional designation, and holds that certification.

PLANSPONSOR.com

PLANSPONSOR.com is the nation's leading online resource for pension and retirement issues.

The site provides comprehensive news, content, and commerce services (via its 401k Pathfinder search service), dedicated to helping employers navigate the complex world of retirement plans on behalf of their employees.

PLANSPONSOR.com's sister publication, PLANSPONSOR Magazine, has been providing authoritative coverage of the US pension industry for nearly a decade. PLANSPONSOR.com's NewsDash e-mail newsletter service is the industry's top daily news digest.

PLANSPONSOR.com is owned and operated by Asset International, Inc., headquartered at 125 Greenwich Avenue, Greenwich, CT. 06830. Asset International also publishes Global Custodian Magazine and GLOBAL-CUSTODIAN.com, which provide industry-leading coverage of the international securities services industry.

This book, along with other books, are available at discounts that make it realistic to provide them as gifts to your customers, clients, and staff. For more information on these long-lasting, cost-effective premiums, please call John Boyer at 800-272-2855 or e-mail him at john@fpbooks.com